MW00784497

Champagne & Sparkling Wines

by Fran Flynn & David Stevens-Castro
Photography by Fran Flynn

PAIRED – Champagne & Sparkling Wines

Published by Paired Media a division of Latino Cellar
9 Woburn Place, Burleigh Waters, QLD 4220, Australia

First Published by Paired Media 2015

Editor Martine Lleonart

Wine facts reviewed for accuracy by Tyson Stelzer

Graphic Design © Frangipani Creative

National Library of Australia Cataloguing-in-Publication Data

Title	PAIRED – Champagne & Sparkling Wines: The food and wine matching recipe book for everyone/ by Fran Flynn & David Stevens-Castro; with foreword by Tyson Stelzer.
ISBN	9780994348500 (hardback)
Series	Paired; volume 1
Subjects	Food and wine pairing Sparkling wines Champagne (Wine) Food Cookbooks

Dewey Number 641.22

Printed by 1010 Printing International Limited, China.

IMPORTANT Those who might be at risk from the effect of salmonella poisoning, i.e. the elderly, pregnant women, young children and those suffering from immune deficiency diseases should consult their doctor with any concerns about eating food containing raw eggs, alcohol, marinated fish and cheese made with unpasturised milk.

CONVERSION GUIDE You may find cooking times vary depending on the oven you are using. For fan-forced ovens, consult your oven user manual for recommended adjustments.

volume 1

PAIRED

Champagne & Sparkling Wines

by Fran Flynn & David Stevens-Castro
Photography by Fran Flynn

Sabrage *is a dramatic technique for opening a bottle of champagne with a sword (sabre) for ceremonial purposes, which originated in the Napolean era.*

CONTENTS

'I have long admired David's enthusiasm for wine, his passion for sparkling and his well-considered touch in aligning wine and food...'

FOREWORD

The world of sparkling wine is fast on the move. Globally, sparkling wine consumption is increasing at twice the rate of still wine. From tiny growers to large houses, wineries are introducing new cuvées (blends). The result has been ever-rising access to the greatest diversity of exciting sparkling styles that the world has ever seen. From the refreshing elegance of prosecco to the reverberating complexity of mature vintage champagne or the rumbling depth of South Australian sparkling shiraz, the grand panorama of sparkling colour is a mighty spectacle to behold.

Once the darling of the aperitif and the cocktail party, a broader variety of fizz has ushered in a new age in which sparkling wine is popped at any hour of the day and sidled up alongside every course from breakfast to dessert. There are sparkling wines out there to match virtually anything you can conjure in the kitchen.

Matching bubbles with the right dish can be one of the most thrilling culinary experiences of all. But getting it wrong can let down both the wine and the food. Fizz can be one of the most elegant and subtle of all beverages and its vast diversity of incarnations calls for careful consideration of the right cuvée to sit alongside a dish.

It's here that David Stevens-Castro and Fran Flynn come to the rescue. I have long admired David's enthusiasm for wine, his passion for sparkling and his well-considered touch in aligning wine and food. He puts this to great effect in his presentation as a sommelier, in social media and now, for the first time, in this book, carefully partnered to Fran's enticing recipes. Their suggestions touch on all the classic pairings and more than a few daring combinations along the way. There's a lot of fun to be had trying these combinations for yourself! This book is a useful guide as you navigate the wonderful world of fizz and food.

Tyson Stelzer

IWSC TROPHY 2015 COMMUNICATOR OF THE YEAR

International Wine & Spirit Communicator of the Year 2015
International Champagne Writer of the Year 2011

David Stevens-Castro is a highly regarded wine expert originally from Chile. He has a degree in Agricultural Science, specialising in fruit and wine production, and extensive experience as a sommelier. Fran Flynn is an award-winning commercial photographer and graphic designer originally from Ireland.

Living together on the Gold Coast, in Australia, they have pooled their skills as a husband-and-wife team to publish this series of books and share their expertise in the things they love.

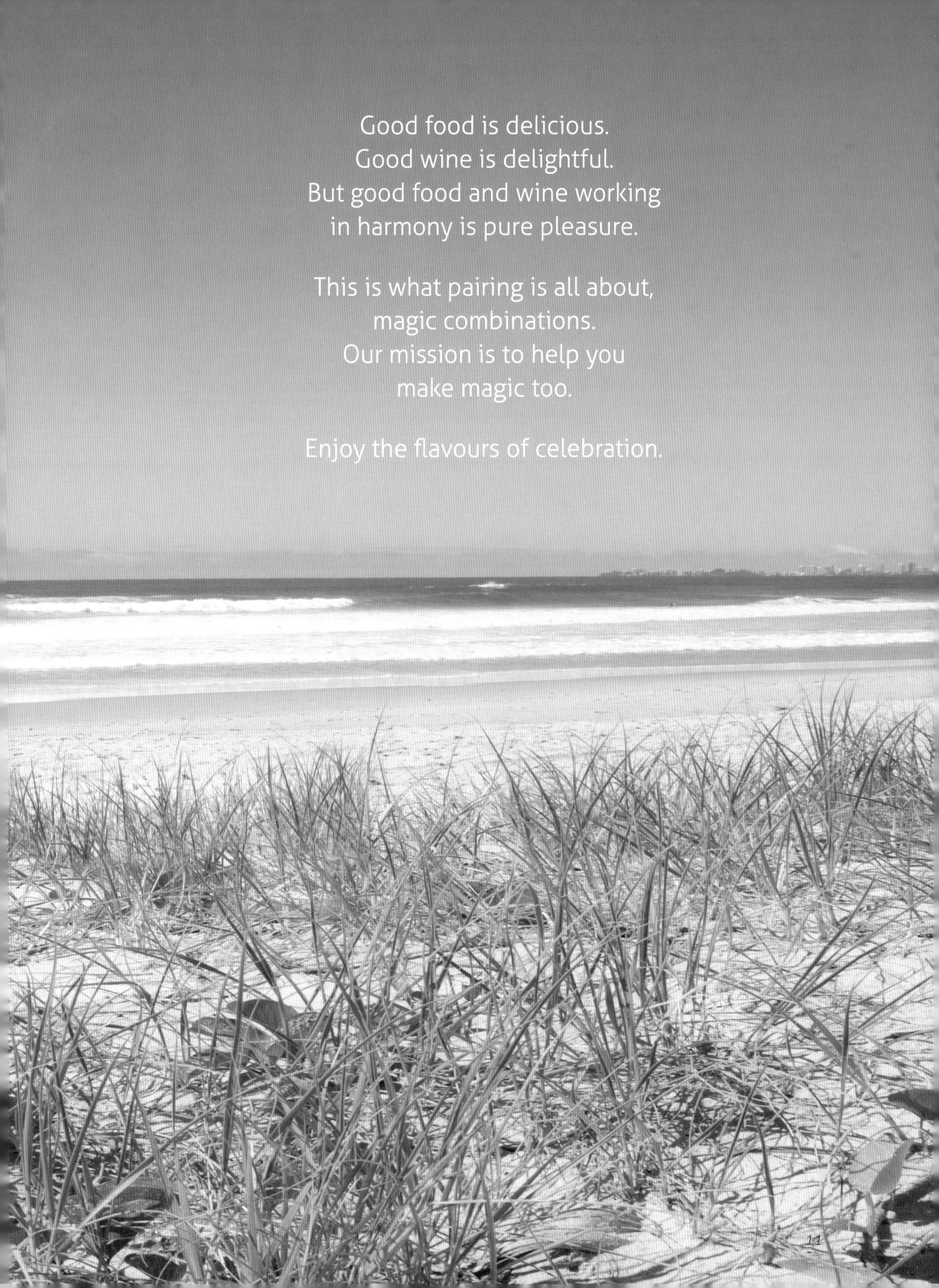

Good food is delicious.
Good wine is delightful.
But good food and wine working
in harmony is pure pleasure.

This is what pairing is all about,
magic combinations.
Our mission is to help you
make magic too.

Enjoy the flavours of celebration.

INTRODUCTION

PAIRED – *Champagne & Sparkling Wines* is the first volume in a series of books that collectively will result in a comprehensive guide for matching all commonly available styles of wine (sparkling, whites and reds) with great recipe suggestions.

This is not a text book, although we hope you will learn something that you didn't know before. PAIRED – *Champagne & Sparkling Wines* is intended to take pride of place on your coffee table as well as make many visits to your kitchen. We hope that it will encourage you to try new things, experiment with fresh flavour combinations and share them with your friends and loved ones. This book is full of simple, achievable dishes that are combined with comprehensive knowledge to help you present with an ideal wine partner.

The selection of recipes is very personal. They draw on our culinary experiences from both of our birth countries, Chile and Ireland, and our collective travel experiences, plus, of course, the diversity of influences in our home continent of Australia. Some dishes might sound ambitious, but everything has been personally home-cooked, tested and tasted multiple times, as well as on-shoot. So if we can do it, we're sure you can too.

Champagne and sparkling wines are often the drinks of choice for special occasions; therefore they sometimes lend themselves to be paired with dishes that may not be considered everyday options. If a dish is a little challenging and an easier option exists, we offer that as an alternative, or we have created a method to make it easier than you might expect.

Your feedback is of great interest to us and all suggestions, likes and dislikes, and constructive criticism is hugely appreciated. We welcome your comments and suggestions, especially for future volumes, which are currently in production. See page 141 to connect with us and to sign up for our newsletter. You can keep informed of when future volumes become available and receive pre-release discounts.

We hope you enjoy reading PAIRED – *Champagne & Sparkling Wines* as much as we have enjoyed putting it together.

INTRODUCING PAIRING

Matching food and wine is an exciting but ambiguous art. Sometimes combinations are inarguably the perfect marriage. More often, personal tastes and individual preference have a significant role to play. Sometimes flavours that could initially be perceived as hopeless bed-fellows turn out to be ideal companions and a beautiful surprise.

Throughout this book we've tried to give you a sense of both: some obvious favourites and some nice surprises. Fran contributes an introduction to each dish, while David offers ideas for pairing and explains why each recipe connects with the suggested wine.

Cheese and wine are renowned for their harmonious relationship and in each chapter we have suggested a cheese that can be particularly well suited to matching with the topical wine.

Food and wine matching is a fun pastime to indulge in as part of a celebration with friends. We recommend you use one of the menu suggestions we have created on page 130, or put together your own selection, using a series of dishes from different chapters. Then invite your friends to each bring a specific bottle of wine to suit the various dishes. The ensuing conversations and sharing of opinions will bring a new dimension to your gathering and can be enjoyed by everyone. We've been lucky enough to enjoy several similar occasions putting this book together.

RESULTS OF PAIRING

We have determined that there are five key results to look for when combining food and wine: cleansing, complementing, paralleling, counterbalancing and enhancing.

Cleansing
A rich, creamy, spicy or heavily flavoured meal can tire or overwhelm the palate very quickly. Introducing a wine with crisp acidity will cleanse the palate between mouthfuls, keeping the meal fresh and enjoyable.

Complementing
When you are eating a dish with a specific flavour, for example strawberries, and then you drink a wine that also expresses this flavour, e.g. a sparkling rosé, the connection between the complementary flavour in both the food and the wine accentuates that flavour and gives it an added dimension.

Paralleling
When a recipe actually contains some wine as an ingredient, and you consume the same wine in a glass, at the same time – this is a parallel match. For example, cava (sparkling wine from Spain) sorbet, moscato (sweet sparkling wine from Italy) cupcakes, white wine sauce, etc. In these cases, the bridge between the food and wine is very discernible.

Counterbalancing
If a food or wine displays an extreme of flavour or aroma, a pairing partner can counterbalance the intensity, creating a sense of equilibrium and harmony.

Enhancing
The ultimate result of pairing is when the marriage of the food and wine brings the flavours to a new level that neither element could achieve alone, and creates a whole new flavour. An excellent example of this is champagne and oysters.

AT A GLANCE

SPARKLING WINES OF THE WORLD

While everyone has, of course, heard of champagne, there is also a broad range of sparkling wines produced worldwide in a variety of styles and flavours. In this book we have focused on the seven main types and categorised them as follows:

CHAMPAGNE *page 30*

France

Champagne is the royalty of all sparkling wines. It is a carefully crafted high quality product that comes from a specific region called Champagne in France. Blends are created using three grapes varieties: chardonnay, pinot noir and meunier. To have 'champagne' on the label, the wine must adhere to strict growing and production regulations, which means that you can be assured of quality control during production. Due to the labour intensity involved, champagne is very much a premium product.

In terms of style, it is possible to find champagne across the full spectrum of flavours, from very sweet to very dry, from light to full bodied, fresh and young to aged and complex. Champagne houses have spent vast amounts of money over centuries carefully refining their product to be the best that it can be. Brands are also very intensively developed and maintained to reflect the prestige of the product. With such a huge span of history, there is no close competitor to the real thing – champagne.

CAVA *page 46*

Spain

Cava originated in the Catalan region of north-east Spain, but nowadays it is licensed in eight regions of Spain. It is usually produced from a combination of three native grapes: macabeo, xarel·lo and paralleda, using very similar methodology to champagne and also under strict regulations. The result is typically either light and zesty or a dry and toasty style, and usually leans to the dry rather than sweet side of the scale.

PROSECCO *page 60*

Italy

Prosecco hails from the Veneto region of Italy. Originally it was perceived to be a cheap sweet wine, but it has evolved to become a light and refreshing dry sparkling, with flavours of apple and pear. Other countries also produce a prosecco-style wine but you can be sure it is has been produced in Italy under regulation if it has DOCG printed on the label.

NEW WORLD SPARKLING *page 74*

Argentina, Australia, Chile, New Zealand, USA

The 'New World' generally refers to winemaking regions outside of the 'original' European domain. Argentina, Australia, Chile, New Zealand and the US are all considered New World producers. In more recent times the UK, India and China have become New World producers also. There can be a perception that New World wines are a lower quality, cheaper offering, however, there are many expertly made wines of maturity. A large proportion of New World sparkling wines are dry, with a soft fruity style and light fresh flavour.

CRÉMANT (CREAMY)

Sparkling wines produced in France outside of the region of Champagne are often categorised as crémant. *Also produced under strict production criteria,* crémant *has a lower fizz level giving it a very creamy sensation. There are eight regions in France licensed to produce* crémant *and one in Luxembourg. Most blends involve chardonnay, chenin blanc and cabernet franc, although certain additional grapes are permitted.*

Crémant *is a lovely sparkling style to sample. In broad terms you could consider champagne pairing guidelines appropriate to* crémant *also.*

SOUTH AFRICA

While South Africa is sometimes also categorised as a New World wine region, it was actually planted earlier than other New World areas. The signature style is known as cap classique and is produced under the traditional method using the same grape varieties as in champagne.

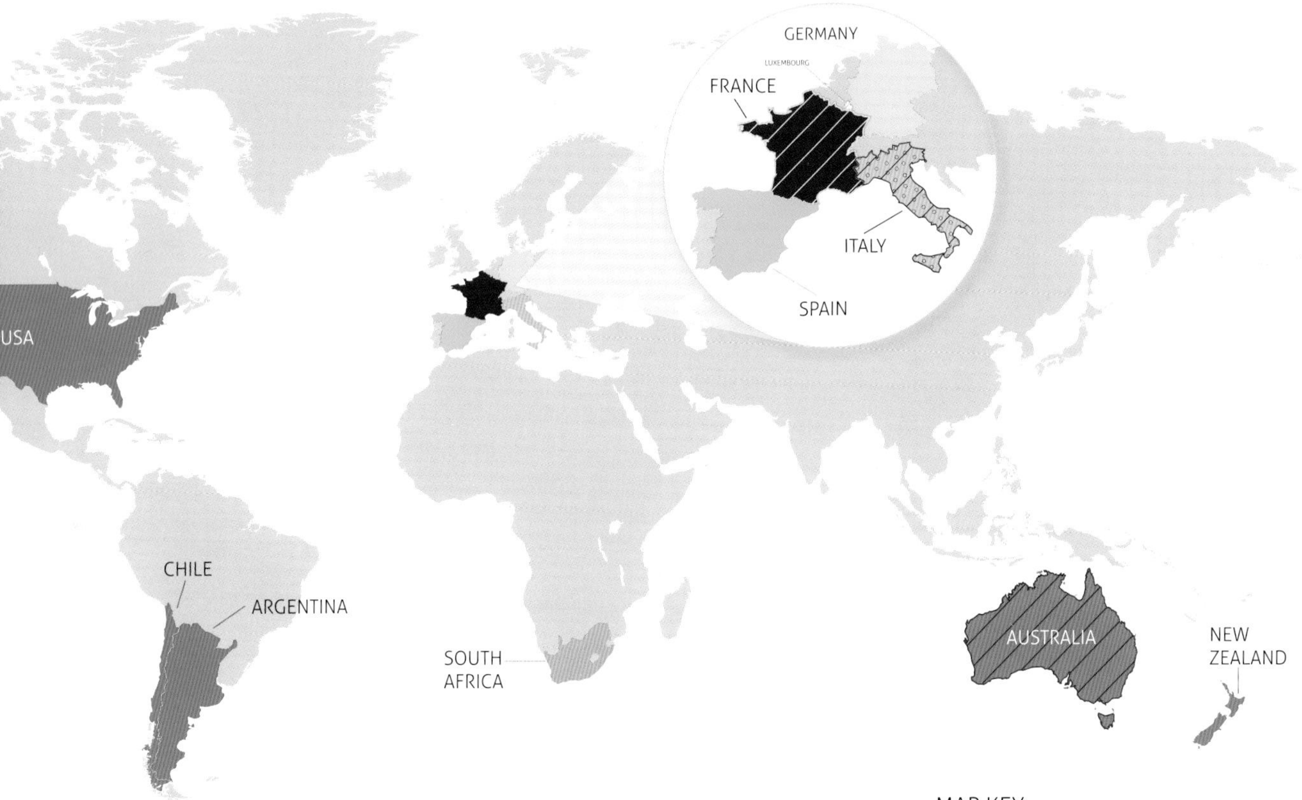

MAP KEY

- *Cava*
- *Cap classique*
- *Champagne*
- *Crémant*
- *Moscato*
- *New World sparkling*
- *Prosecco*
- *Sekt*
- *Sparkling red*
- *Sparkling rosé*

SPARKLING ROSÉ *page 88*

Most countries that produce sparkling wine

The majority of sparkling wine regions also produce sparkling rosé. Most notable would be from Southern France, Northern Spain, Italy and New World regions including Western USA. The style can range from very dry to semi-sweet, depending on the producer and terroir.

MOSCATO *page 102*

Italy

'Moscato' is the Italian word used to describe wine made from the muscat grape. While most moscatos are lightly sparkling there are many non-sparkling examples also. A typical sparkling moscato would be sweet and low alcohol with a white or pink colour and a unique Turkish-delight aroma.

The classic sparkling moscato is made under careful regulation in Italy and is called Moscato d'Asti, from the region in which it is produced. Australia, Southern France and the US are also known for their sparkling and non-sparkling muscat offerings.

SPARKLING REDS *page 116*

Australia, Italy

Australia has put considerable effort into developing respected sparkling reds, particularly from the shiraz variety. The style is generally quite rich in flavour and is sometimes slightly sweet or, more often, off-dry. There are also other varieties available including cabernet sauvignon, merlot and petit syrah. Italy produces the majority of other red sparklings, with lambrusco being the best known. Lambrusco is produced in a broad variety of styles. Another sparkling red Italian option is Brachetto d'Acqui, which is generally quite sweet with low alcohol.

OTHER SPARKLINGS

We have selected a range of sparkling wines to showcase in this book, however there are many other variations throughout the world. Other options include sekt and secco from Germany and franciacorta from Italy. It is also possible to find offerings from countries as diverse as Hungry, Portugal, Romania, Russia, Switzerland and even the UK, produced from both imported and homegrown grapes.

UNDERSTANDING THE LABEL

The tricky thing about buying champagne and many sparkling wines is understanding what exactly is in the bottle. The information on the label can be quite difficult to understand unless you are already 'in the know'. A guide to decipher the meaning is essential – and here it is!

CLASSIFICATION OF SPARKLING WINE

Despite common misconception, 'champagne' is not a grape variety; it is a region with a very regulated growing environment and production characteristics. Champagne is usually made from a blend of specific grapes – chardonnay, pinot noir and meunier – and the blend can consist of wine that has been stored from different years of growth. Other sparkling wines often emulate champagne as closely as they can.

Prestige Cuvée or Cuvée Spéciale (Cuvée means 'blend')
This often indicates the highest quality product that a winery has to offer from their collection, with the blend including the coveted 'first juice' of the pressing (i.e. pristine juice, unsullied by pulp, seeds or skin). However, unless it actually says 'Prestige Cuvée' or 'Cuvée Spéciale', which is a regulated classification of quality, anything else is usually just a pretty name. For example, don't be fooled by 'Fantastic Cuvée' or 'Cuvée Amazing' – the word cuvée alone usually just means 'blend'.

Vintage
Vintage sparkling requires that – depending on the location – between 85% and 100% of the blend must have been produced from a single harvest of grapes, grown during a year recognised as exceptional. Champagne requires 100% from a single harvest. Vintage sparkling wines are often of a high quality and therefore suitable for cellaring, particularly vintage champagne.

Non-vintage (NV)
The majority of champagne and sparkling wine produced is non-vintage. This means that the blend can be made from juice from harvests of multiple years. If the bottle doesn't say 'vintage' on the label, or state a year, you can presume it is a non-vintage wine.

Reserve
This can be a confusing term because it should usually refer to wine that has had at least a portion of the blend 'reserved' for aging because it is of particularly good quality. Unfortunately, in many countries there is no regulation around the term and it can be used as a misleading marketing ploy.

Blanc de blancs
This term means 'white from white' and indicates a sparkling wine made solely from white grapes, usually chardonnay.

Blanc de noirs
This means 'white from black' and refers to the fact that the sparkling white wine has been made from red wine grapes, e.g. pinot noir or meunier. This is achieved by removing the juice with minimal skin contact (which is the source of the colour), therefore producing a light colour.

Rosé sparkling wine or champagne rosé (also known as pink champagne)
This can be created from one of four methods, however, it is most often coloured by adding a small amount of red wine from pinot noir or meunier to the mix, which gives the characteristic pink colour and distinctive flavour.

AOC/DO/DOC/DOCG etc
*Many wines are produced under strict regulations to ensure quality. These are usually defined within a geographical zone.
In English this is known as PDO – Protected Designation of Origin. Each language has a different acronym for essentially the same thing, i.e. French AOC, Spanish DO/DOCa, Italian DOC/DOCG, German QbA/QmP, etc. If you see one of these acronyms on a label you can feel assured that the product meets strict requirements to achieve a high standard of quality.*

TERROIR
This is a special term used to encompass the environment, soil type, growing conditions and climate during grape growing for wine.

FERMENTATION
In the case of wine production, fermentation refers to the process of converting grape juice into alcohol by using yeast to convert natural sugars in the juice into alcohol.

Example of a 'translated' high quality label. Note all *this information would rarely appear on one label.*

Grapes in this wine come from one of the top 17 villages in the Champagne region

Most or all of the grapes were grown in 2002, and 'vintage' means from a year recognised for superior quality

Brand, sometimes well known

Comes from the Champagne region in France

Made from chardonnay or other white grapes

Extra brut is the driest style that exists

The highest quality blend that this house offers

Might be made from grapes that are considered particularly good, and the juice has been held aside to age and develop for a while, or it's just a marketing ploy.

SWEET TO DRY

When sparkling wine was first produced sweet examples were the favourite, but fashion changes and currently it's predominantly all about dryness. Moscato is the only style that is always sweet. The sweetness level also has a major impact on the flavour and consistency of the wine and therefore what it can be matched with in terms of food. See below for sweet to dry range.

WINEMAKING METHOD

Méthode traditionnelle (also known as traditional method or classic method)
This is the term used for the production process utilised to make champagne. After the grapes are pressed, the juice initially ferments in large vessels and then, after the winemaker has created a blend, it experiences a second fermentation in the bottle. This method produces a smooth, creamy result with small, delicate bubbles. Sparkling wines that use this method include cava, American sparkling wine and some Italian and New World offerings.

Transfer method
Similar to the traditional method, until the final stage, when some processes are completed more economically in large vessels rather than the more labour intensive process of the second fermentation occurring in the bottle.

Charmat method
During both fermentations the wine is stored in less labour intensive stainless steel tanks, rather than in individual bottles like the traditional method. It tends to produce a fruitier result, with less refined bubbles.

Injection method/carbonation
Sparkling wine that has had the bubbles added with CO_2 – as opposed to as a result of fermentation – are generally of a lower quality.

BODY

This refers to how the consistency of the wine is affected by the viscosity of alcohol. This is described as light, medium or full-bodied.

It can be compared to how the difference in texture between skimmed, whole and creamed milk feels in the mouth.

SWEET TO DRY RANGE

Extra brut – Very dry
Brut – Dry
Extra dry – Off-dry
Sec – Lightly sweet
Demi-sec – Sweet
Doux – Very sweet

GRAPE QUALITY

The locations where champagne grapes are grown are divided by village with a rating system called Échelle des Crus, which means 'ladder of growth' or, more simply, the Crus Scale. Grapes grown in the villages at the top of the scale can demand the highest price for their grapes.

Grand Cru
The very best of the Crus Scale is a champagne created from one of the top 17 (i.e. less than 9% of planted area in Champagne) rated villages in Champagne. These are classified as Grand Cru.

Premier Cru
Coming a close second are champagnes classified as Premier Cru quality. The remainder of Champagne villages are just referred to as Cru. A traditional use of the French word 'cru' in champagne means growth.

Everywhere else around the world, the best quality sparkling wines will come from locations that have been identified as having especially favourable conditions. This is often referred to as 'single vineyard' on a label, to emphasise the quality and limit of availability for that wine.

TYPES OF BUBBLES

Many people think that the bubbles in sparkling wines are added by carbonation, like a soft drink, however it's actually usually a result of natural reactions brought about during the fermentation process, although carbonation is used sometimes in cheap sparkling wines. Each winemaking method produces different types of bubbles.

The traditional method generally creates a small, delicate bubble, with a smooth, creamy texture that usually lasts the longest. The *transfer method* produces a similar bubble, although not as long lasting. *The charmat method* results in a larger, more effervescent but less refined bubble. *Carbonation* also produces a large bubble.

BRANDING

The reputation of a champagne house is often enough to sell its product, so most houses put serious effort into the quality and presentation of their products. Traditionally many houses have been built by families who have passed the business from generation to generation, maintaining the integrity of the product and also the brand. However, these days most of the major players are owned by big corporations.

Sparkling wine producers are also keenly aware of the importance of brand presentation and substantial money, time and effort is poured into standing out from the crowd.

SERVING & STORAGE

TEMPERATURE

Champagnes and sparkling wines are often served too cold and the flavours are dulled as a result. In general, sparkling wines should be served between 8°C (46°F) and 12°C (53°F). As a broad rule of thumb it is usually advisable to serve the better quality champagnes at the warmer end of the scale to experience the full depth of flavour, and the younger, or non-vintage offerings, at the cooler end of the scale.

When you have served the first pour make sure to quickly return the bottle to continue chilling. It will lose correct temperature very quickly if left unrefrigerated. In very warm climates you can remove the bottle from chilling at a lower than ideal temperature, because by the time it reaches the glass it is likely to have warmed in the process of the bottle opening and serving.

Use a wine stopper to prevent loss of the essential effervescence. Don't bother with the 'teaspoon' technique, it's purely a concept of fiction. A proper sparkling wine stopper is cheap and easy to find.

OPENING

Sabrage is the ultimate opening technique, when a sword is used to dramatically sabre the cork and neck of the bottle. It's best to leave this technique to the professionals though! The most important thing to remember when opening a bottle of sparkling wine is to always hold your thumb over the cork. Sparkling wine is bottled at very high pressure and an unbridled cork can cause injury. Most bottles come with an easy-open tab to peel the foil. Then you untwist the wire (with your thumb over the cork) and, finally, gently turn the bottle while holding the cork – rather than vice versa. You should ideally hear a subtle 'hiss' rather than experience a big explosion...unless you're keen on the drama.

POURING

Angle the glass to allow the wine to slide down the side and prevent over-bubbling and spillage. Allow the foam to settle and then top up to a comfortable height. Avoid filling the glass too high as this leaves no space for air to interact with the wine – or distance between the bubbles and the nose of the recipient. About two-thirds full is the ideal measure.

GLASSWARE

While the typical champagne flute is the most obvious choice for your sparkling wine, using a larger white wine glass can sometimes enhance the experience of a particularly expressive offering. Even if you do stick with a champagne flute, not all glassware is the same, and different diameters of rim can have a big impact on the way you experience the beverage. Try an experiment by pouring the same wine into a few glasses with different rim diameters and see if you can notice a difference.

There are three main styles of champagne glass: coupe (or champagne saucer), champagne flute and champagne tulip.

The distinctive wide, shallow bowled coupe looks very elegant and is a classic image that you will see in many Hollywood movies. Unfortunately, despite its attractive appearance, it's not the ideal glass for drinking sparkling wine from, because the bubbles disperse very quickly and can leave you with a flat drink, unless you're drinking quite fast, plus it's very easy to spill.

In a standard eatery, the flute is the glass that you are most likely to be served sparkling wine in. The tall narrow shape retains the effervescence well and rapidly funnels the flavours and aromas. While it looks great and works well with younger sparkling wines, more expressive vintage examples can be best served in a wider rimmed glass to facilitate better delivery.

Finally, the tulip glass is recommended as the ideal by many professionals because the shape of the bowl allows a bit more interaction with air before the wine is delivered, offering a bit more expression than a flute.

coupe *standard flute* *tulip* *trumpet bowl flute* *long stemmed flute*

CHEESE PAIRING

Cheese and wine have a very special affinity, particularly due to similarities in the positive effect aging has on flavour. Furthermore, there is huge choice and variety in both wines and cheeses, giving you a broad array of options to try. Experimentation is highly recommended.

The quality and flavour of wine and cheese are both determined by a combination of environmental factors in addition to a cheese or winemaker's methodology. The old adage 'what grows together goes together' is very true for wine and cheese and you will commonly find natural, complementary pairings of wine and cheese from specific regions.

Just like wine, older cheeses have more developed, savoury flavours and younger cheeses tend to be lighter and fresher. There is logic then, in pairing older cheeses with older wines as they are less likely to be overwhelmed by the cheese's flavour.

Similarly, certain flavours that can be associated with older wines also tend to appear in many aged cheeses, i.e. earthy, nutty, rich and more intense characteristics than their younger counterparts.

When we consider sparkling wines specifically, the lighter, fresher options – such as a youthful champagne or cava, prosecco, and NV sparkling rosé – comfortably complement fresh soft young cheeses. They all match well with creamy brie, chèvre (creamy goat's cheese) and fresh ricotta.

A very important consideration with brie and camembert, however, is the rind. A thicker, slightly fluffy style of white cheese rind doesn't pair well with sparkling. You are looking for a French-style cheese that is almost rindless and creamy. Mozzarella is also really not a friend of sparkling wine.

When contemplating semi-hard cheeses, overall they will tend to pair well with the more complex flavours of vintage champagnes and vintage New World sparklings; a mild cheddar pairs with all the white sparkling wines except for prosecco. Gouda however is more difficult to match, and is only recommended to pair with prosecco, cava and moscato.

Of course, perfect pairing isn't as simplistic as this, but it's a good place to start. To add another element into the equation we can consider the happy affinity between saltiness and sweetness. Some cheeses can be particularly salty, and sweeter wines counterbalance this beautifully. For example, blue cheese can be quite salty and, surprisingly, marries well with a lambrusco or sparkling shiraz.

Another strong pairing opportunity with acidic sparkling wine is the cleansing effect. If you are eating a creamy or flavoursome cheese, selecting a wine that can offer a 'cleansing' style of match will mean that your palate will be refreshed and won't be tired or overwhelmed by the flavour. Brie is a great example of this.

Of course, the circumstance will eventuate when you would like to offer a variety of cheeses and you only want to open one bottle. In this situation, if you choose your cheeses carefully, a sparkling rosé will be the most versatile. A cava or champagne would be next in line for flexibility.

TASTING WINE AND CHEESE

Take a piece of cheese in your mouth. Chew for long enough to get a good sense of the flavour. Taste the wine. Swish it around your mouth to blend with the cheese and get a full appreciation of the flavour combination. Finally, after swallowing the cheese, take one final mouthful of wine to enjoy the effect with the residue of the cheese.

BASIC FOOD PAIRING

There are classic pairings for sparkling wine that are universally known and loved for their compatibility, e.g. champagne and oysters. However, sparkling wines are more versatile than they are generally given credit for and can be paired with a surprisingly broad range of flavours.

Sparkling wine can be considered a versatile style of wine for pairing and there is no reason why you can't enjoy champagne and sparkling wines with every course of a meal.

Probably the most important characteristic to be mindful of when pairing food with sparkling wine is the scale of sweetness to dryness. As a generalisation, brut (dry) examples are going to suit a broader range of flavours than sweet sparkling wines. Dry champagnes and sparklings are best suited to buttery, oily and sometimes creamy partners (like a light, creamy seafood pasta), whereas sweet wines usually work best to complement desserts and fruits. See page 19 for the dry to sweet scale.

The chart opposite is a starting point, but by no means a definitive guide. Pairing isn't a science, it is an adventure in flavours that can sometimes surprise. Matching food and wine can be perceived as daunting, however, once you can allay concern for making unpalatable mistakes, it's really fun.

We have created a series of recipes that include many of the ingredients suggested on the facing page for you to experiment with. It's very important to remember that adding or subtracting one significant component to a dish can change the whole flavour profile, so the best way to be sure that your intended combination is going to sing harmoniously is to taste test. Piccolo-sized (200ml, 7fl oz) bottles can be very useful for trialling new ideas. Your taste buds are the best judge of what works. You'll find that everyone has different preferences, but some combinations are just so good they excite everyone.

As a broad guideline:

- Buttery, lightly creamy and oily dishes are a lovely counterbalance to dry champagne and sparklings, for example, seafood/shellfish with a light cream-based sauce.
- The acidity of dry champagne or sparkling wine cleanses the palate between mouthfuls, helping to refresh the senses for the next bite.
- Eggs in most formats are a great companion of champagne and sparklings. Consider quiche, scrambled eggs and even pancakes.
- Gently spicy food, particularly Asian-style dishes, work well with sparkling wine, especially rosé, because the acidity cools off a mild heat from the spiciness and the rosé accentuates the flavours.
- Salty foods can be nicely balanced by champagne, for example, salty cheese, popcorn and potato chips.
- Avoid sweet desserts with a very dry sparkling. Instead, a sweet sparkling can work well, or even try a mid-level demi-sec.
- While pasta is generally a great friend to sparkling wine, tomato sauce is usually a no-no, unless paired with a sparkling red.

TASTE TESTING

Food and wine matching is a very subjective art. One person's pleasure can be another person's poison.

We have tasted and tested all the matches and recipes that are suggested in this book, and feel confident suggesting them as great companions.

Having said that, we are also 'breaking the mould' with some of our ideas and there will be those that don't agree with all of our suggestions. We relish the opportunity to create conversation, learn from other opinions, and also to be challenged to try new combinations ourselves.

For example, we enjoy the cleansing effect of a sparkling wine with gently spicy food, but someone else might find the food too dominant.

We consider chocolate to be a beautiful accompaniment to champagne and sparklings but it is not a traditionally accepted pairing.

The most important thing that we'd like to encourage is experimentation. There is no 'correct' formula. Taste test as much as possible, try the unexpected and enjoy developing your opinions based on your own experiences.

Important: *Identify the dominant flavour of a dish before attempting to pair, e.g. a chicken dish with a rich creamy or tomato sauce has a dominant flavour based on characteristics of the sauce, not the chicken.*

KEY
No dot = Not a match
Black dot = Ideal match
Other dot = Good match

	FOOD GROUPS	CHAMPAGNE	CAVA	PROSECCO	NEW WORLD SPARKLING	SPARKLING ROSÉ	MOSCATO	SPARKLING RED
CHEESE	blue cheese				◐		◐	◐
	creamy goat's cheese	◐	◐	◐	◐	◐	◐	
	double cream brie*	●	●	●		◐	●	◐
	fetta/queso fresco			◐		◐		◐
	gruyère & jarslberg		◐		◐	◐		
	halloumi	◐	◐	◐	◐	◐		
	light Swiss	◐	◐		◐	◐	◐	
	mild cheddar	◐	◐		◐	◐	◐	
	manchego	◐	●		◐	◐		◐
	ricotta	◐	◐	●		◐		◐
	vintage hard cheese	●	◐		◐	◐		◐
MEAT/EGGS	charcuterie	◐	◐		◐	●		◐
	chicken	◐	◐		◐	◐		◐
	duck	◐				◐		●
	eggs	●	◐	◐	●	◐	◐	◐
	ham	◐	◐		◐	◐		◐
	lamb					◐		●
	pork cutlet	◐	◐			●		◐
	prosciutto	◐	◐	◐	◐	◐		◐
FISH	calamari	◐	◐	◐	◐	◐		
	caviar	●	◐	◐	●	◐		
	ceviche	◐	◐	◐	◐	◐		
	oysters	◐	◐	◐	◐	◐		
	shellfish	●	◐	◐	●	●		
	smoked salmon	●	◐	◐	●	◐		
	sushi	◐	●	◐	◐	◐		
VEGETABLES	asparagus (thin)	◐	◐	◐	◐	◐		
	mushrooms	◐	◐	◐	◐	◐		◐
	pasta	◐	◐	◐	◐	◐		◐
	plain olives				◐	◐		
	potatoes	◐	◐	◐	◐	◐	◐	◐
	salad	◐	◐	◐	◐	●	◐	◐
	spring onions (scallions)	◐	◐	◐	◐	◐		
SWEETS	berries	◐	◐	◐	◐	◐	◐	●
	cheesecake	◐	◐	◐	◐	◐	◐	◐
	chocolate	◐	◐	◐	◐	●	●	●
	cupcakes	◐	◐	◐	◐	◐	◐	◐
	fruit sauces	◐	◐	◐	◐	◐	●	◐
	shortbread	◐	◐	◐	◐	◐	◐	◐
	sorbet	◐	◐	◐	◐	◐	◐	
FLAVOURS	buttery	◐	◐		◐	◐	◐	
	fried, oily	◐	◐	◐	◐	◐		
	light creamy	◐	◐	◐	◐			
	mild chilli/gently spicy		◐			◐		
	nutty	●	◐	●	●	◐	◐	
	popcorn	◐	◐	◐	◐	◐		
	salty	◐	◐	◐	◐	◐		

*Please refer to note on cheese rind, page 23

WHAT ARE THE DIFFERENCES?

Soil structure affects grapes, weather affects grapes, topography affects grapes, winemaking technique manipulates grapes, and everything affects flavour! As a result there can be significant differences between all the variations of sparkling wines. In order to create this brief overview generalisation has

STYLE	WHERE IT'S PRODUCED	GRAPE VARIETIES USED	PRODUCED UNDER REGULATION	METHOD (See page 19)
Champagne	Only in the Champagne region of France. Grapes are grown in chalky soil with some clay and sand at high latitude (meaning low temperatures).	Predominantly chardonnay, pinot noir and meunier.	Yes, grapes must be hand harvested, grown in the defined geographical zone of Champagne, blended with specific grape varieties, grown under strict viticulture controls and use methodé traditionnelle for production.	Methodé traditionnelle
Cava	Only in Spain. It originated in Penedès, Cataluna, in the north of Spain. Grapes are grown in coastal regions with low temperatures and breezy nights.	Predominantly Spanish white varieties, parellada, xarel·lo, and macabeo, but several other varieties are permitted including chardonnay.	Yes, the selection of grape varieties and method of production are regulated aspects of cava production.	Traditional method
Prosecco	Veneto and Friuli Venezia Giulia in Northern Italy. Cool climate mountainous region with high altitude and low temperatures produces crisp high acidity wines.	Glera. Nine other grapes are permitted to make up 15% of the blend.	Yes, it must be produced within the defined geographical zone of Northern Italy and follow certain production methods. Other countries also produce sparkling wine using the glera grape, and will even call it prosecco, however the letters DOC or DOCG on the label verify it as a real Italian prosecco, produced under full regulation.	Charmat method

been necessary. It's also worth bearing in mind that often, the higher the price the better the quality. A poor quality example can unfairly put you off a whole genre, so it's generally worthwhile purchasing the best that you can afford – although being pleasantly surprised by a cheaper offering is a pleasure.

SWEET/DRY	ACIDITY	ALCOHOL	STYLE OF BUBBLE	FLAVOUR PROFILE	PAIRING
Usually brut/ extra brut (dry/ extremely dry), although sweeter champagnes are also available.	High	11–13%	Fine bead with a creamy mousse.	Champagne often has the aroma of a freshly opened tin of sugar shortbread biscuits. A youthful champagne has a flavour that can give a similar experience to the crunch and zest of fresh nectarines or strawberries, and a mature example will usually have nutty/toasty characteristics also.	Champagne is the most sophisticated of all sparkling wines. It has fresh crispy flavour with depth, and is versatile for pairing with a broad range of foods, especially seafood, a broad variety of cheeses, eggs, fried food and the majority of buttery, oily dishes and nutty flavours.
Dry	High, but not as high as champagne	12–13%	Fine bead with a creamy mousse, but not quite as fine as champagne.	Good cava has some similarities to champagne, so it can also exhibit biscuity aromas, however it is fruitier, and can express scents of white peach or lilies also. It has a slightly tropical fruit flavour, and it is a bit soft and juicy, rather than mineral and dry like champagne.	Cava has enough similarities to champagne that it will usually pair successfully with foods that work well with champagne also. Highly recommend purchasing cava from Penedès, and the best that your budget can afford, because the difference can be dramatic. Ideal food partners include manchego cheese and sushi.
Varies from brut, extra-dry or sec (lightly sweet) – it is more fashionable these days to be dry, whereas in the past it was known for sweetness.	Medium +	11–12%	Broad, i.e. larger bubble/ less fine than champagne.	Prosecco has a crisp, light, fresh flavour – picture eating green apples and pears while nibbling almonds – and also with similar aromas.	Prosecco is well suited to light dishes, salads and fresh produce, nothing too heavy. It can also match well with mushrooms, some risotto, and chicken. It's not as versatile as some of the other categories, and pairing needs to be done more carefully.

STYLE	WHERE IT'S PRODUCED	GRAPE VARIETIES USED	PRODUCED UNDER REGULATION	METHOD (See page 19)
New World Sparkling	Argentina, Australia, Chile, New Zealand and the US among others. Cool climate regions predominantly resulting in citric flavours. The proximity to sea and/ or high altitude gives additional vibrancy in flavour and aroma.	Varies but most try to emulate champagne in some way so favourite varieties are chardonnay, pinot noir and meunier. Riesling, pinot grigio, and chenin blanc also feature sometimes.	No, there is no specific obligation to follow any rules other than localised requirements. Reading a label carefully will give more detail on variations.	Traditional method Charmat method Transfer method Injection method
Sparkling Rosé	In all regions around the world that produce sparkling wine, e.g. Argentina, Australia, Chile, Europe, New Zealand and the US, with mainly cool climate conditions.	Pinot noir, meunier, and to a lesser extent chardonnay. Theoretically any grape can be used as long as at least one red grape is included, although the above are generally the favoured choices.	No, there are no specific obligations to follow any rules other than localised requirements. Reading a label carefully will give more detail on variations.	Traditional method Charmat method Transfer method Injection method
Moscato	Moscato d'Asti – Piedmont, Italy Also high altitude, cool climate area, with calcium-rich soil. Moscato Style – Australia, Spain, US	Muscat Moscato-style wines from outside of Asti use other grapes also.	Yes and no. It originated in Piedmont, Italy, and is produced under regulations as moscato d'Asti in this region. However, a variation, described as 'moscato-style' is produced in other locations without regulation.	Charmat method
Sparkling Red – Lambrusco	Italy, Emilia-Romagna	Lambrusco	Lambrusco is produced under regulation. It has many sub-varieties and eight are permitted to be used in the production of lambrusco wines.	Traditional method Charmat method
Sparkling Red – Shiraz	Mainly Australia (South Australia and the Great Western Region, Victoria)	Shiraz and other less dominant varieties including cabernet sauvignon, merlot, pinot noir and petit syrah.	Sparkling shiraz has no specific obligations besides local requirements.	Traditional method Charmat method

SWEET/DRY	ACIDITY	ALCOHOL	STYLE OF BUBBLE	FLAVOUR PROFILE	PAIRING
It varies from country to country and wine to wine, but generally dry.	Medium +	11–12%	Depends on production. The more time consuming traditional method creates a finer, longer lasting bead than other methods. See page 20.	Often the flavour of New World sparklings are fruitier than champagne, with fruity aromas, and can have a taste reminiscent of fresh vanilla or pineapple ice-cream.	While New World sparklings are generally less expensive and therefore usually less finessed than champagne, they are often attempting to emulate champagne and therefore tend to match with similar dishes. For example, many cheeses, seafood, shellfish, eggs, pasta and light poultry are suitable.
There is a broad spectrum available from sweet to dry, however, the drier end of the scale is currently much more fashionable.	Medium +	11–12.5%	Broad, i.e. chunkier or less fine than champagne except in the case of champagne rosé.	With a sparkling rosé, visualise fruity and concentrated flavours of strawberries and cream (but not too sweet), with an aroma of red cherries.	Sparkling rosé is a versatile option for pairing, and can work with a broad range of dishes, as well as matching well with many desserts. Best partners are charcuterie, shellfish, duck, berries and chocolate.
Sweet	Very low	Mocasto d'Asti max. 5.5% Moscato Style variable, usually around 5%	Delicate bubble.	Moscato often smells like sweet talc or perfume and has a yummy Turkish delight flavour. Typically soft yellow in colour it can also be presented with a pink colour.	Moscato is quite different to other sparkling wines in that it is usually very sweet and low in alcohol. It is mainly suited for aperitif or desserts and is lovely with many cheeses, ice-cream, and sweet treats, plus light savoury dishes like salad.
Off-dry to slightly sweet but usually sweeter than sparkling shiraz.	Low	11% +	Lightly sparkling with a big bubble and a purplish mousse.	Slightly sweet, light, fruity, inexpensive, everyday drinking, with flavours of berries.	Lambrusco pairs well with salami and cured meats, tomato-based sauces and pizza as well as red fruits/ desserts.
Off-dry to slightly sweet.	Low	12–14%	Big bubble.	With an aroma like boiled plums and blackberry jam the flavour is rich and dry.	Sparkling shiraz is most enjoyable with duck, pork and lamb and pairs especially well with berries and chocolate and is even popular with a bacon and eggs breakfast.

Oysters with caviar & foam 38

Gnocchi with asparagus & butter sauce 40

Goat's cheese parcels 42

champagne

CHAMPAGNE

Benedictine Monks can be congratulated for blessing the world in the 1500s, quite by accident, with the glorious beverage that we now know as sparkling wine. In fact, at the time the bubbles were seen as an undesirable fault and great efforts were made to try to eradicate them.

As tastes developed in favour of bubbles, winemakers still struggled to control the process and prevent the so-called 'Devil's Wine' from regularly exploding weak bottles and causing a chain reaction of destruction in the cellar.

By the 19th century, bottles had progressed enough to withstand the pressure, and the fermentation process was properly understood, leading to the champagne industry as we now know it.

Nowadays in 250km (155 miles) of cellars and tunnels that run underneath the towns and villages of the Champagne region, millions of bottles of champagne are carefully stored in ideal conditions. The value of these collections runs into billions of dollars.

Blend
Over many years, grapes harvested in Champagne are categorised and stored as fermented juice in separate vats. When winemakers are ready to create a new blend, they have access to this large collection of resources to blend from. A standard *non-vintage* blend can include portions of the three main grape varieties – chardonnay, pinot noir and meunier – and within these varieties, examples from multiple years.

The winemaker creates the finished blend almost like a perfumier creates a perfume. Everything is meticulously noted so the same result can be reproduced consistently.

A *vintage* blend will use grapes from a harvest that has been recognised as exceptional. The grapes must be aged for at least three years and the blend must include 100% of grapes from this one growing season. However, grapes from the three key varieties can still be utilised in the blend if desired.

Making the champagne
Fermentation is the natural process used to convert grape juice into alcohol. In the case of champagne, which follows the traditional method (methodé traditionnelle), the grapes are first pressed to release the juice. The juice then usually has yeast cultures introduced to provoke fermentation and spends several days in a tank. Subsequently, the winemaker creates their blend of juice, along with sugar and yeast, and transfers this mix into bottles. A second fermentation then occurs within the bottle.

Over a period of time, the bottle is moved onto different angles to allow sediment to release and settle, until it forms one sticky mass. Ingenuously, when the time comes, this is removed by holding the bottle upside down, which allows the sediment to settle at the opening of the bottle. Then the bottle is momentarily frozen and unsealed, and the pressure of the CO_2 (carbon dioxide) forces this 'plug' out as one unit. The wine is then resealed and ready for distribution. This process is called 'disgorgement'.

Main im
Monthelon, Champagne, Fra
© Michel Guillard/Collection

L
Champagne cellar, Re
© Michel Guillard/Collection

Disgorging by h
i.e. releasing the sedim
from a champagne bo
© Photo Collection

Light rail in Re
© Shutters

Pruning the v
© Shutters

CHAMPAGNE

QUICK REFERENCE

LOCATION
Champagne region, France

GRAPES
Chardonnay,
pinot noir, meunier

REGULATIONS
Strict viticulture and
production requirements

WINEMAKING METHOD
Methodé Traditionnelle

ACIDITY High

ALCOHOL 11–13%

IDEAL PAIRING
Especially seafood, selective cheeses, fried food and the majority of buttery, oily and lightly creamy dishes

PAIRING CHAMPAGNE

We have already discussed the basics of pairing in the previous section. To take it a step further, we need to recognise that often there are other variations to be considered.

Champagne has four key styles: blanc de blancs (made from chardonnay or other white grapes only); blanc de noirs (made from red grapes only, either pinot noir or meunier); a blend (which will usually have a combination of all three varieties), and; last but not least, rosé. Additionally, each of these styles can be further divided by vintage or non-vintage examples, i.e. vintage meaning that all the grapes have come from one exceptional harvest year and non-vintage meaning that the grapes used in the blend can be a mixture from two or more years. Furthermore, the level of dry to sweet should be considered. Overall this might seem quite complicated, but the chart on the facing page simplifies everything to make it easy to understand.

Champagne universally matches beautifully with a variety of cheeses, many fish and shellfish, as well as buttery and lightly creamy dishes and biscuity flavours. Dry vintage blanc de noirs and dry vintage blends, which have additional richness and complexity, marry particularly well with slightly rich, oily, fried, nutty and lightly creamy dishes.

Sweeter (demi-sec) vintage blends are ideal for a light creamy chocolate dessert, as well as foie gras and fragrant or gently spiced Thai food.

Champagne rosé has some particular characteristics that make it more appropriate to refer to pairing tips in the chapter dedicated to sparkling rosé (page 88). It can handle the oily flavours of duck and pork, and will also pair beautifully with charcuterie, salad and chocolate.

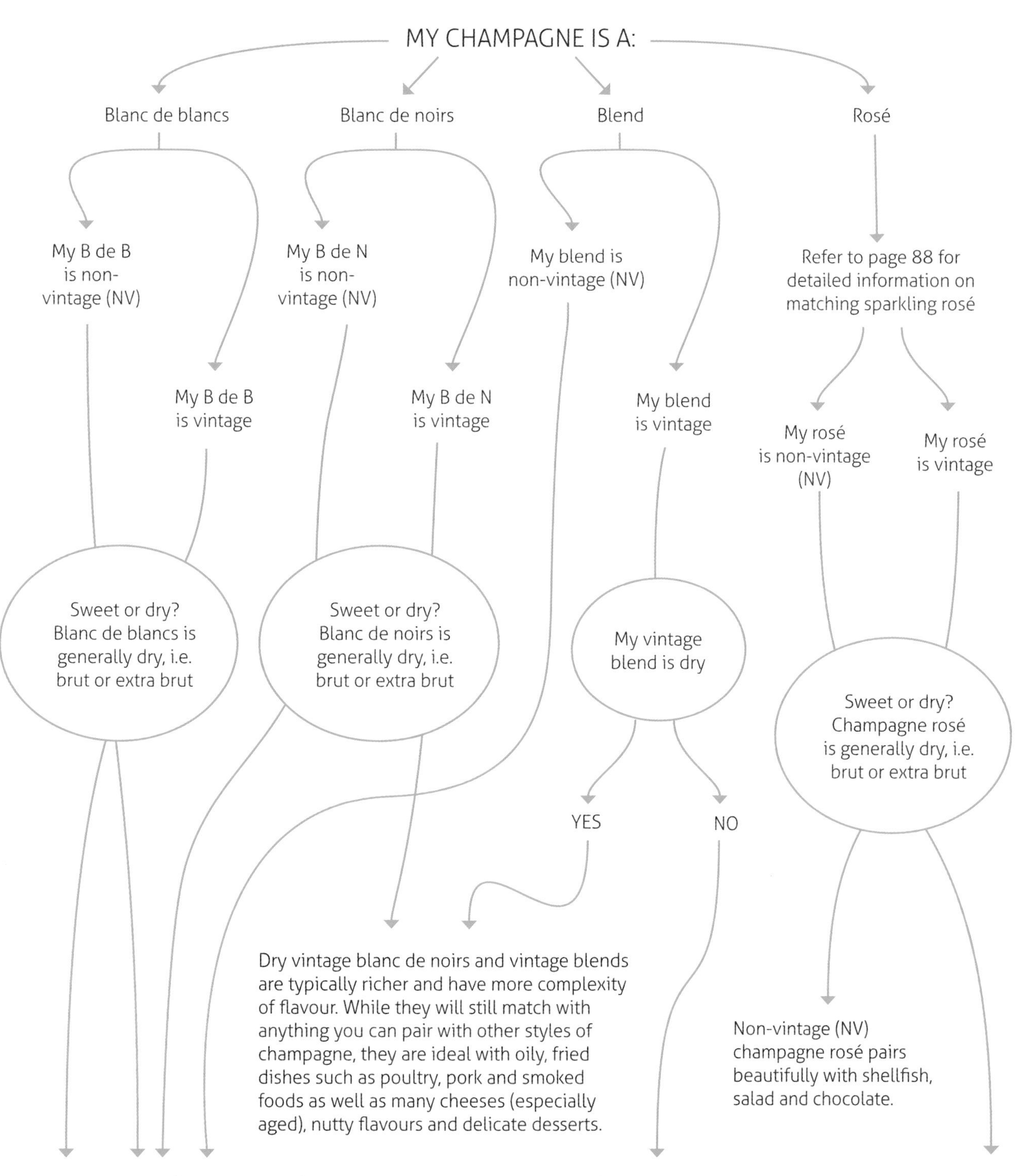

MY CHAMPAGNE IS A:
Blanc de blancs
Blanc de noirs
Blend
Rosé
My B de B is non-vintage (NV)
My B de B is vintage
My B de N is non-vintage (NV)
My B de N is vintage
My blend is non-vintage (NV)
My blend is vintage
Refer to page 88 for detailed information on matching sparkling rosé
My rosé is non-vintage (NV)
My rosé is vintage
Sweet or dry? Blanc de blancs is generally dry, i.e. brut or extra brut
Sweet or dry? Blanc de noirs is generally dry, i.e. brut or extra brut
My vintage blend is dry
Sweet or dry? Champagne rosé is generally dry, i.e. brut or extra brut
YES
NO
Dry vintage blanc de noirs and vintage blends are typically richer and have more complexity of flavour. While they will still match with anything you can pair with other styles of champagne, they are ideal with oily, fried dishes such as poultry, pork and smoked foods as well as many cheeses (especially aged), nutty flavours and delicate desserts.
Non-vintage (NV) champagne rosé pairs beautifully with shellfish, salad and chocolate.

Blanc de blancs (vintage and NV), blanc de noirs NV and a dry vintage blend all have light fruity characteristics. The blanc de noirs NV is a bit richer, but all these variations pair well with cheese, shellfish, seafood, fish, canapés and salad.

Sweeter champagne (usually demi-sec) is not particularly fashionable at the moment, but you can still find examples. Ideally paired with foie gras, fragrant Thai food, light creamy chocolate and sweet/fruity desserts.

Along with matches that work for NV champagne rosé, vintage rosé – with more richness and complexity – will pair beautifully with charcuterie, duck, pork and chocolate.

cheese *match*

You can never have too much cheese! Next to chocolate it's my favourite food infatuation. When it comes to matching with champagne, many cheeses can work. Matching the age and style of the cheese with the right type of champagne is the key. For example, some soft creamy cheeses like chèvre (light creamy goat's cheese) are beautiful with a young fresh NV champagne. Older vintage champagne has the character and strength to complement more flavoursome, older cheeses such as parmigiana-reggiano, pecorino, manchego and aged cheddar.

Serving suggestion

Consider trying chèvre on crusty French bread with a non-vintage champagne, ideally a blanc de blancs. Add fresh figs for a lovely, gentle touch of sweetness.

OYSTERS
with caviar & foam

Caviar isn't always ridiculously expensive and foam isn't as tricky as it looks! Before you discount this as an elitist dish that you'd never consider trying yourself, give it a go – it'll definitely set the scene with the 'wow' factor on a special social occasion and it tastes sensational. Lumpfish caviar can be found inexpensively in small jars in many supermarkets and is totally sufficient for this presentation. The foam is a simple mix of a few easy ingredients.

Prep 15 min
Serves 4

Ingredients

a dozen freshly shucked oysters, very chilled

coarse sea salt for presentation

black caviar

Foam

piccolo (200ml/7fl oz) champagne or sparkling wine

2 x separated egg whites at room temperature

half a lemon, squeezed

Method

Source the freshest oysters you can find. Look for beautiful undamaged shells. It would be ideal to shuck them yourself, but we prefer pre-shucked because it can be quite a challenging – not to mention dangerous – task.

In a mixing bowl whisk wine, egg whites and lemon juice – ideally with a stick blender – for about four minutes, or until the foam is holding. Note: you don't have to use the same wine as you are drinking, a cheaper product is sufficient as long as it doesn't have an overbearing flavour.

Using a small dish per person, place three very chilled oysters on a bed of coarse sea salt. Make sure that each oyster is released to slide easily from the shell. Add a couple of drops of filtered/bottled water to each oyster. Carefully place a teaspoonful of caviar on the lip edge of each oyster shell.

Gently add a heaped teaspoonful of the freshly whisked foam on top of the caviar. Don't wait around to eat this one: the foam will drop quickly – it needs to be served and consumed immediately, so make sure that your guests' glasses are charged and ready to go.

Pairing

The most enjoyable part of this matching is the creamy mousse sensation of foam and champagne together, contrasted by the crunchy caviar and the delicate saltiness of the oysters. A blanc de blancs champagne (which is chardonnay-based – read more page 35) is a lovely match because it is subtly citric but also substantial and very fresh, so it doesn't overpower the exquisite combination of flavours. Such a nice aperitif!

Suggested match

Champagne, ideally blanc de blancs

PAIRING STYLE / ENHANCING

Caviar isn't always expensive and foam isn't as tricky as it looks

GNOCCHI
with asparagus & butter sauce

This can be a very quick simple recipe if you choose to use ready-made gnocchi, but the satisfaction you can derive from successfully creating your own handmade light fluffy gnocchi is an experience worth having, and it can be surprisingly fun and easy too. If you opt for the former option, try to find freshly made gnocchi with natural ingredients.

Shop gnocchi	*Homemade gnocchi*
Prep 10 min	*Prep 60 min*
Cook 8 min	*Cook 45 min*
Serves 4	*Serves 4*

Homemade gnocchi ingredients

1kg (2lb 3oz) floury potatoes (russet or king Edward are ideal)

2 cups (300g/10½oz) 00 Italian flour, or plain (all-purpose) flour, sifted

1 packet coarse sea salt

Gnocchi method

The key to light gnocchi is potatoes with a low water content that have been dehydrated as much as possible, which is why we opt to oven-bake rather than boil the potatoes for this dish.

Clean and dry the potatoes with their skins on and pierce liberally. Place in a preheated oven on a bed of coarse salt at 220°C/425°F for approximately 40 minutes or until they can be pricked with a fork without resistance, but not too soft that they start to break up. Allow to cool. Remove skins and rice the potatoes using a potato ricer. If you don't have a ricer, using a flat cheese grater can be quite successful – just grate it very gently to break it up into small fluffy crumbs.

Weigh the potatoes and measure out 1 cup (150g/5oz) flour per 450g (1lb) riced potato. Gradually work together about two-thirds of the flour and all of the potato on a floured benchtop – ideally blending with a bench scraper or similar tool – until it peels from the board without stickiness and has a nice light doughy consistency. Roll the dough into an even sausage about 2.5cm (1 inch) in diameter and cut into evenly spaced bite-sized 'pillows'. Finally, turn each piece on it's side and imprint the gnocchi with a floured fork to texturise and make oval in shape. Set to one side until ready to complete the dish.

To cook: place gnocchi carefully in boiling salted water and cook for a few minutes until they start to float. Remove immediately with a straining ladle.

Asparagus sauce ingredients

2 bunches asparagus

2 heaped tablespoons olive oil spread (butter substitute)

1 lemon

salt & pepper

2 tablespoons pine nuts, toasted

parmesan cheese, small block

small bunch fresh chives, trimmed

Method

Cut the asparagus into thirds after discarding the woody end of the stem. In a lightly greased pan, on a high heat, fry the gnocchi until golden and set aside. Melt the spread in the pan and add the asparagus. Add a tablespoon of water and cover with a large saucepan lid to retain humidity. Toss regularly until asparagus becomes a bright green and the texture is al dente.

Return the gnocchi to the pan and combine with the asparagus. Remove from the heat. Add a generous squeeze of lemon juice, salt and pepper and sprinkle with toasted pine nuts.

Grate some parmesan with a vegetable peeler for the garnish, and sprinkle with fresh chives.

Pairing

Perfectly cooked gnocchi is lightly rich and melts in the mouth without chewiness. The lovely oiliness of the butter sauce adds to the fullness of the flavour. Vintage champagne has chalky high acidity that can cleanse the palate between mouthfuls, keeping the dish fresh. I recommend a vintage blend because it is flavoursome enough that it won't be overwhelmed.

Suggested match

Champagne, ideally a vintage blend

PAIRING STYLE / CLEANSING

GOAT'S CHEESE PARCELS

This is one of my favourite recipes in the book. The delicate crispness of the filo pastry gives way to a smooth, lush, crunchy texture with a surprise burst of grapes to enliven the senses. These may look tricky, but they are actually easy, quick and fun to make. Goat's cheese can be pricey but it's worth it for a special occasion. You can experiment with other cream cheeses, just make sure you review your wine match if you do. With a milder cheese, it's a good idea to add an additional peeled grape to each parcel for extra flavour.

Prep 45 min
Cook 10 min
Yield 10–12 parcels

Ingredients

1 heaped tablespoon olive oil spread or butter
1 packet/375g (13oz) filo pastry, thawed
180g (6½oz) light creamy goat's cheese
12 seedless grapes, skinned and quartered
3 spring onions (scallions), very finely sliced
large handful of slivered almonds, toasted
fresh thyme
freshly ground black pepper
kitchen twine and scissors to tie parcels

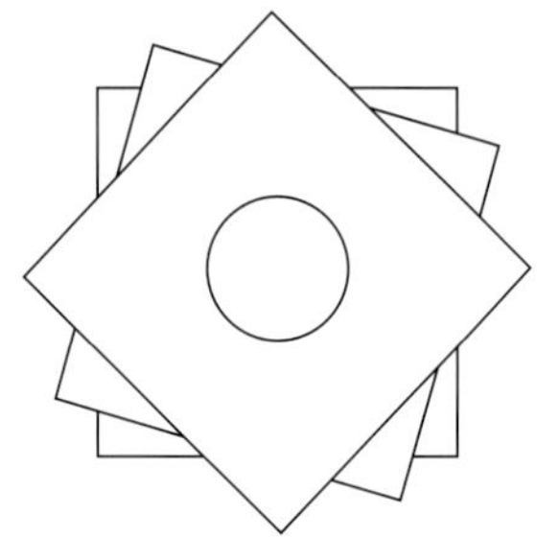

Fig. 1. Proportions of filling to parcel sheets

Method

Preheat oven to 200°C/400°F. Melt the butter/olive spread in the microwave or in a saucepan and transfer to a bowl. Cut the filo pastry into squares approximately 20cm (8in) and divide into groups of three sheets. Lay the first three sheets on a board, and angle them to make a star shape. Brush the top sheet generously with the melted butter. Place two thin slices of goat's cheese in the centre and one grape per parcel and sprinkle with remaining ingredients including thyme leaves, stripped from the twigs. Be careful not to overfill. Proportions should look like fig.1.

Cut a length of twine. Draw all the corners of the pastry to the centre and pinch into a parcel. Tie very gently with the twine and twist a sprig of thyme into the bow. Brush with butter.

Place on baking paper in a baking tray and repeat. When all your parcels are ready, bake in the oven for 10 minutes, or until golden brown. Serve immediately.

Pairing

The intense flavour of goat's cheese can be hard to counterbalance. The richness of a vintage blanc de blancs champagne (see page 35) with its striking salty and mineral acidity, works in harmony with the creamy texture of this delicious cheese. It also enhances the surprising mix of sweet, crunchy and herbal elements. There is so much to enjoy in this match made in heaven. Truly delightful.

Suggested match

Champagne, ideally vintage blanc de blancs

PAIRING STYLE / ENHANCING

Many people think *that the bubbles in champagne are added by carbonation, like a soft drink, however it's actually a result of natural reactions caused by the fermentation process, i.e. when added yeast causes the natural sugars in the grape juice to convert to alcohol.*

Spicy prawn tapas 52

Ceviche
(citrus marinated fish) 54

Cava sorbet with
lemon & orange juice 56

cava

CAVA

Cava originated in Penedès in the Catalan region of north-east Spain in the 19th century. The Spanish learnt about sparkling wines because the corks used for French champagne were being sourced from Spain. Tentative attempts to produce wine using the same methodology followed and quickly evolved to award-winning standard. Late in the 19th century, a nasty aphid-like louse called phylloxera wiped out most of the French vineyards, giving Spain a great opportunity to increase their exports and establish cava as a popular beverage. By the time the louse reached Spain a workable solution had been found and phylloxera was less of a threat.

The 1960s saw the introduction of regulations to define the quality and methodology of cava production, giving greater credibility to the name cava.

Winemaking
While 95% of cava is produced in Penedès, there are eight other regions within Spain that are also allowed to produce cava under Spanish law. The main grapes used are local varieties macabeo, xarel·lo and parellada, however chardonnay, pinot noir, garnacha and monastrell can also be used. Cava follows the traditional method, which is the same process used for champagne production. This is a key regulation for cava production. Additionally, rules about grapes varieties, method of growing, location of vines and other stipulations combine to define authentic cava.

Cava is also blended using a similar methodology to champagne. The winemaker carefully utilises differing proportions of the permitted grapes and varying years of vintage to create a unique blend. Automation has been introduced to many processes, which allows for a cheaper product to be produced, arguably without substantial loss of quality.

Pairing cava
Cava is generally dry (brut), or extremely dry (extra brut). There are three key styles of cava: non-vintage, vintage/aged and rosé. When attempting a food match, cava rosé can be considered similar to other sparkling rosé, so we recommend that you refer to the relevant chapter on page 88. Most cava tends to match well with typical Spanish fare such as manchego cheese, paella, tapas, eggs and seafood.

A non-vintage cava has a typically dry, light, fresh, fruity style and pairs particularly well with salads, pasta, rice and Thai food. Aged non-vintage cava is referred to as 'reserva' or 'gran reserva' to identify aging for a minimum of fifteen or thirty months respectively.

Vintage cava is aged and only uses grapes from a year that has been recognised as having had ideal growing conditions that have resulted in exceptional grapes. Aged cava has the best grapes held aside for aging, but not from a year recognised for excellence.

A vintage cava, or a cava that has been aged for more than fifteen months, has dry, nutty, creamy and toasty characteristics that can match beautifully with the same suggestions as for NV, plus especially with nutty, oily or fried foods. It also pairs well with saltiness such as salty cheese, potato chips and fish, or even meats, like pork or duck.

Main im
Vines in winter, Penedès, Sp
© *Pamela McCre*

L
Col·legi de Sant Jo
Vilafranca del Penedès, Sp
© *Maria Rosa F*

Tower of peo
Santa Rosalia festi
Torredembarra, Cataluña, Sp
© *Josep Santa*

Vineyard, Penedès, Sp
© *Angelina*

La Boqueria Mark
Barcelona, Sp
© *Shutters*

CAVA

QUICK REFERENCE

LOCATION
Spain

GRAPES
Macabeo, xarel·lo and parellada

REGULATIONS
Strict viticulture and production requirements

WINEMAKING METHOD
Traditional method

ACIDITY High

ALCOHOL 12–13%

IDEAL PAIRING
Especially seafood, cheeses, fried food, lightly creamy dishes and the majority of buttery, oily recipes.

cheese *match*

Background

Manchego is a famous cheese, made from sheep's milk in the La Marcha region of Spain, which can be found all around the world. It pairs beautifully with cava. There are three distinctive styles of manchego: young, cured and aged. Younger manchego is semi-soft and moist with a tangy flavour. As the cheese matures the flavour becomes stronger and nuttier and the texture firmer. An aged manchego is likely to have a darker colour and crumbly texture.

Serving suggestion

All cava will go with manchego, but for the optimum result, try to match the age of your cheese with the age of the wine, i.e. if your cheese is quite young go for a NV cava, but if it is an aged cheese try a vintage cava. To complement the nutty characteristics of both the wine and the cheese, you can enjoy manchego cheese and cava served with some almonds and walnuts.

Ingredients

2 tablespoons butter

1 tablespoon oil

½ cup finely chopped onion

75g (2.5oz) flour

100g (3.5oz) manchego cheese – ⅔ coarsely grated & ⅓ finely grated

1 cup (250ml/8.5fl oz) milk

75g (2.5oz) serrano ham or bacon pieces, finely chopped

2 large eggs, lightly whisked

120g (4.5oz) breadcrumbs

bonus recipe

MANCHEGO CHEESE CROQUETAS

Method

Grease a large saucepan with oil and melt butter. Add onion and stir until softened. Over a medium heat, gradually add flour, coarsely grated cheese and milk. Stir continuously until cheese is all melted and consistency is like mashed potato. Add ham and mix until evenly distributed.

Spoon onto a sheet of foil on a plate, cool for a few minutes and then close the foil over the mixture. Cool for at least an hour in the fridge.

Set up three bowls, flour in one, eggs in the second and breadcrumbs mixed with finely grated cheese in the third. With floured hands, shape an oval ball from a portion of mixture and dip it briefly in eggs and then breadcrumbs. Lay it onto a clean sheet of foil. Repeat until all the mixture is shaped.

Heat a deep fryer to 190°C/375°F. Cook croquetas for two minutes each until golden brown and crispy on the outside. Remove with a straining spoon and blot on paper towels. Serve warm.

Prep 30 min
Cooling 1 hr
Cook 8 min
Serves 12–15 croquetas

SPICY PRAWN TAPAS

with melon & cucumber

Spicy prawns (shrimp) are a top choice for a Spanish tapas-style cava match. This recipe was actually a spontaneous creation on a visit to my family in Ireland, when I volunteered to cook the Sunday roast. I wanted to make an Australian-influenced starter, hence the prawns, but I was also influenced by the fact that traditionally my Dad used to always serve melon for a starter with the Sunday roast when I was a child. The chilled sweetness of the melon and cucumber counterbalances the spiciness of the prawns beautifully.

Prep 15 min
Cook 3 min
Serves 4

Ingredients

32 raw, fresh or defrosted prawns (shrimp), shelled and deveined

1 melon, very ripe honeydew or cantaloupe

1 cucumber, skinned and seeded

paprika (preferably non-smoked)

Method

Thread four prawns onto a skewer. Repeat, allowing two skewers per person.

Scoop melon into half-moon shapes using a melon scoop or teaspoon, or cut into bite-sized cubes. Shave ribbon lengths from cucumber with vegetable peeler.

Heat a frying pan with a tablespoon of oil. Generously coat one side of the prawn skewers with paprika. Fry over a sizzling heat (coated side down) for 1½ minutes or until prawn starts to colour/curl.

Coat the second side of the prawn skewers with paprika on the pan and then flip, cooking for another minute or until ready. Place the prawns on top of a bed of melon pieces. Decorate with cucumber ribbons and a small drizzle of oil. Include any paprika 'chips' from the pan as a garnish. Serve immediately.

Pairing

The fresh fruity flavour of Spanish cava works in synergy with the contrast of the sweetness of the melon and the spiciness of the prawns. The lively and crispy combination could lead you to momentarily drift away and contemplate a Mediterranean lifestyle!

Suggested match
Non-vintage cava

PAIRING STYLE / COUNTERBALANCE

CEVICHE
(citrus marinated fish)

I discovered the pleasure of ceviche on my first trip to Chile with David. For me it's like the sashimi of South America but with a richer sensation. Having tasted several variations by some fantastic chefs during the trip it was pretty intimidating to attempt to recreate it at home. However, I was very determined that I wouldn't be waiting until the next trip to Chile to experience the pleasure again. It is surprisingly straightforward to make, with the quality and freshness of the fish and timing of the marinade being key considerations.

Prep 10 min
Marinate 20 min
Serves 2 large or 4 small

Ingredients

450g (1lb) of firm, fresh snapper fillets (or other semi-firm white-fleshed fish such as sea bass, sole or flounder), completely deboned, and cut into 1cm (½ inch) pieces

½ cup (125ml/4fl oz) freshly squeezed lime juice

½ cup (125ml/4fl oz) freshly squeezed lemon juice

½ red onion, finely diced

1 cup fresh tomatoes, seeded and finely diced

1 small red chilli, seeded and finely diced

1 teaspoon of coarse sea salt

1 teaspoon mixed herbs (optional)

1 heaped tablespoon fresh coriander (cilantro), finely chopped plus a few leaves to garnish

Method

Place the fish in a bowl and smother with mixed lime and lemon juice. Cover and marinate in the fridge for 10 minutes, then stir carefully to make sure all the fish is properly soaked. Marinate for a further 10 minutes and remove fish from the juices. During the marinating process the fish will change to a white opaque colour with a firm exterior and tender interior. Taste test to check the fish is tender. If necessary marinate for a few more minutes. Marinating for too long will result in the fish starting to break up, so it's important to get your timing right.

Combine the fish with the onion, tomatoes, chilli, salt and herbs.

Serve immediately in small portions, with a side of crackers or toasted bread. For presentation, you can form a dome by pressing one serve into a small bowl and turning it upside down onto a dish. Garnish with coriander (cilantro) leaves.

Pairing

Freshness is everything in this dish. The mousse of the vintage cava (being more delicate than a non-vintage), along with the dry, crisp, fruity finish, works harmoniously with the citrus essence, which is the character of this dish. In Chile this is a favourite on a hot afternoon in summer on the beach, served in little pots. Avocado is an addition that I can recommend.

Suggested match
Cava, ideally vintage brut

PAIRING STYLE / CLEANSING

CAVA SORBET

with fresh lemon & orange juice

This is a fantastic sorbet. It doesn't need to be made over heat or in an ice-cream maker. It does, however, need overnight to set, so plan in advance. It took five attempts to perfect this recipe, but the result is delicious. You can taste the cava, and when it's just made, maybe even sense a little bit of fizz. Using a blender or blending stick is very important to get the consistency correct and also to allow it to freeze properly. The accuracy of measurements is also important.

Prep 10 min plus overnight freeezing
Serves 6–8

Ingredients

2 cups (500ml/17fl oz) water

¾ cup (170g/3½ oz) of caster (superfine) sugar

2 level teaspoons gelatine powder

½ cup (125ml/4fl oz) non-vintage cava

¼ cup (60ml/2fl oz) freshly squeezed lemon juice

¼ cup (60ml/2fl oz) freshly squeezed orange juice

zest of half a lemon (optional)

vanilla essence (optional)

edible glitter (pictured) or gold leaf to decorate

Method

Stir the sugar into the water with a whisk until it is fully dissolved. Add gelatine and stir again until it also dissolves. Add the cava, juices, zest and ten drops of vanilla. Mix well.

Cover and freeze in the coldest part of the freezer for 1½ hours. Remove and stir well with a whisk. Return to the freezer and stir about every 1½ to two hours, two further times. As it starts to freeze, you might need to break up the forming ice crystals with a fork before you can stir. The more you stir, the more air will be incorporated, resulting in a lighter finished product. Wait another two hours, for a final stir. It should be semi-frozen by now, if not, wait a while longer. This time use a blending stick or blender for a couple of minutes, until the mixture changes to a creamy white sorbet consistency. Freeze overnight.

Alternatively, you can use an ice-cream maker for the freezing stage.

To serve, transfer to serving glasses and garnish with edible gold or glitter (or a decoration of your choice). Serve immediately.

Pairing

Since the sorbet already showcases the cava as one of its key ingredients, the intention with this pairing is purely to gently complement. The soft and fruity non-vintage cava adds a delicate, fizzy finishing touch by refreshing your mouth with the same flavour. Make sure to serve the same cava as you have used in the sorbet.

Suggested match
Non-vintage cava

PAIRING STYLE / PARALLELING

What grows together goes together...

The unique characteristics and flavours of grapes are heavily influenced by the environment they are grown in. The same holds true for the flavours of other fruits and vegetables. Even meat can have an environmentally influenced flavour depending on where the stock was raised. Hence, food that is traditionally grown in the same region as a wine is produced tends to be an ideal match.

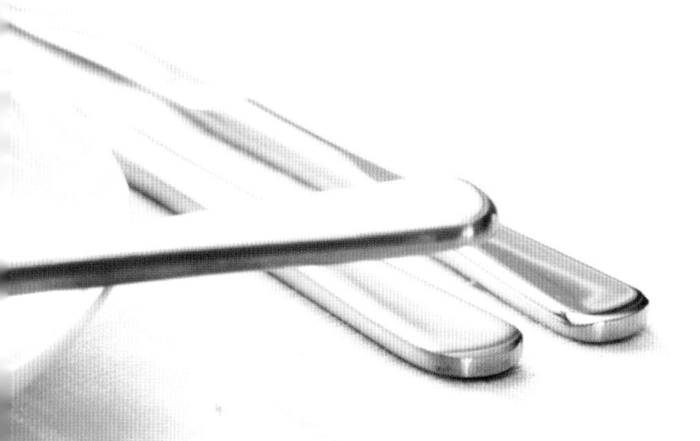

Ricotta stuffed mushrooms with sun-dried tomatoes 66

Chicken tenders with pistachio, almond & parmesan herb crust 68

Apple, pear & caramel parfait 70

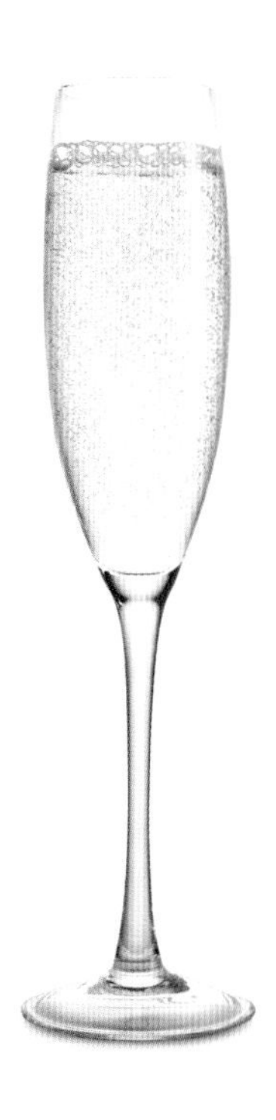

prosecco

PROSECCO

Prosecco is native to the mountainous area of Veneto, Northern Italy. The prosecco grape glera has a history that stretches as far back as Roman times. It was first seen with bubbles in the late 19th century. The defined zone for grape production runs between the two small towns of Conegliano and Valdobbiadene, close to Venice. Vines cling at seemingly impossible angles on the sunny side of slopes where it can be difficult to even stand upright. As a result, hand management and harvesting is the only available option.

Regulations for the cultivation, production and winemaking of authentic prosecco have been carefully maintained by a special consortium charged with safeguarding the quality of the product. True prosecco from this region of fifteen municipalities will have DOC or DOCG on the label, signifying that it has been produced according to the required regulations of the designated zone. Other countries produce wine from the glera grape and attach the name prosecco to their label, but true prosecco only comes from this area. The hill of Cartizze is home to what is considered to be the highest quality prosecco. If a prosecco contains grapes from this area it will appear on the wine bottle label.

Producers are canvassing for the name 'prosecco' to become a legally protected name, just like champagne or cava. If this happens, only wine from this region will be allowed to use the name prosecco.

Winemaking
Prosecco is generally produced using the charmat (tank/martinotti) method, which is a less labour intensive process than the traditional method. For the second fermentation the wine is stored in large tanks rather than individual bottles. This approach retains a lighter, fruitier quality than the more yeasty character of champagne. This wine is designed to be consumed while young and fresh, ideally within a year of the vintage. There is some prosecco that is produced with the secondary fermentation in the bottle. This approach would be indicated on the label as 'traditional/classic method' and adds to the quality and longevity of the wine.

Prosecco has two potential levels of fizziness: either spumante, which is fully sparkling, or frizzante, which is lightly sparkling.

Pairing Prosecco
Prosecco comes in four main styles: dry (brut), extra-dry, sec and demi-sec (semi-sweet). However, the current preference internationally is brut, so you are most likely to find this style.

With a light, fresh, delicate appeal prosecco is best suited to pair with flavours that won't overwhelm and light dishes such as salad and slightly sweet desserts are ideal. Prosecco also has a particular affinity with mushrooms and soft Italian cheeses. It can also pair well with chicken, risotto, sushi and shellfish.

Main im
Vineyard, Valdobbiadene, I
© *Flavio Vallenari / is*

L
Dolomites Mountains, I
© *Shutters*

Venice, Veneto, I
© *Shutters*

Pruning the vi
© *Shutters*

Venice, Veneto, I
© *Kushch Dr*
Shutters

PROSECCO

QUICK REFERENCE

LOCATION
Veneto, Italy

GRAPES
85% glera, plus nine other grapes are permitted to make up the other 15% of the blend

REGULATIONS
Strict viticulture and production requirements

WINEMAKING METHOD
Charmat method

ACIDITY High

ALCOHOL 10.5–12%

IDEAL PAIRING
Dishes that won't overwhelm the light fruity style, such as salad, sushi and light desserts

cheese *match*

Ricotta is a whey cheese, made from the milk of either goat, sheep, cow, or even Italian water buffalo.

The most widely available and familiar style of ricotta is young, light, white, fresh and moist.

There are also aged variations available that are produced by using fresh ricotta and preserving it by salting, baking, smoking or fermenting. These processes can create stronger flavours.

Fresh ricotta is extremely versatile, and is used as a base or ingredient in many desserts, fillings, condiments and savoury dishes.

Do your best to find authentic fresh ricotta. It's a big step above what you can find in a tub.

Ingredients

300g (10.5oz) fresh ricotta cheese

½ garlic clove, peeled and grated

1 tablespoon fresh chives, finely chopped

1 tablespoon fresh parsley, finely chopped

1 tablespoon fresh mint, finely chopped

½ lemon, squeezed

3 tablespoons olive oil

salt and pepper

Prep 10 min

Serves 2–4

bonus recipe

RICOTTA DIP WITH FRESH HERBS

Method

In a medium bowl, mix all of the ingredients together. As you mix, taste test and adjust the seasoning to your palate. Cover and refrigerate for a couple of hours (but no longer) to allow the flavours to meld. Warm to room temperature for half an hour prior to serving.

Serve with Italian crackers like crostini.

STUFFED MUSHROOMS

with ricotta & sun-dried tomatoes

Large juicy portabello mushrooms stuffed with lush, creamy ricotta cheese, paired with a light, fresh prosecco – it's an easy and very pleasurable combination. This dish even sports the colours of Italy, as well as a sense of Italian flavours. It's also an ideal share dish and surprisingly rich too. Usually one large mushroom per person is enough.

Prep 15 min

Cook 20 min

Serves 4

Ingredients

200g (7oz) ricotta cheese, preferably fresh and full-fat

50g (1¾oz) sun-dried tomatoes, finely chopped

1 tablespoon fresh flat leaf parsley, finely chopped

4 large portabello mushrooms

½ small red onion, finely diced

1 garlic clove, peeled and minced

parmesan cheese, coarsely grated

salt & pepper

Method

Preheat oven to 190°C/375°F. Mix ricotta, sun-dried tomatoes and finely chopped parsley in a bowl and put to one side.

Remove the stems of the mushrooms and finely chop. Gently fry with onion and garlic until just softened. Allow to cool slightly and then add to ricotta blend and mix fully.

Re-grease the same pan with a little bit of oil, to seal the mushrooms. Put on a high heat, add a few drops of water and place a large saucepan lid propped at an angle over the mushrooms to increase humidity and prevent drying while frying. Fry for about a minute each side.

Once sealed, place mushrooms in an oven dish on a layer of baking paper and heap with ricotta mix, until all mushrooms have a dome of the ricotta blend on top. Sprinkle with some parmesan.

Bake for 20–25 minutes or until tender. Transfer to a wire tray and top with some freshly chopped parsley, salt and pepper and a little bit more parmesan. Serve immediately.

Pairing

This is a classic example of 'what grows together goes together' with the Italian influence of the dish matching nicely with the Italian wine. A light easy-drinking non-vintage prosecco beautifully cleanses the palate after the richness of the ricotta. The potentially strong flavours of the onion, sun-dried tomato and parmesan are pleasantly restrained by the acidity of the wine.

Suggested match

Dry non-vintage prosecco ideally from Veneto, Italy

PAIRING STYLE / CLEANSING

CHICKEN TENDERS

with pistachio, almond & parmesan herb crust

Oven roasted chicken tenders are quick, easy and yummy, and since they are not fried, they are also a healthy option. Children love to help make them, as well as eat them. The nuts and cheese bring a whole new dimension to a breadcrumb crust, and the tangy dipping sauce adds flavour too. They are very versatile and are a lovely snack, light lunch, shared plate for guests or can be part of a main meal served with salad and vegetables.

Prep 20 min

Cook 20 min

Serves 4

Ingredients

2 large chicken breasts
50g (1¾oz) pistachio nuts
50g (1¾oz) almonds
100g (3½oz) breadcrumbs
1 tablespoon mixed herbs
100g (3½oz) parmesan cheese, finely grated
2 large eggs
1 cup (150g/5½oz) plain (all-purpose) flour

Dipping sauce

100g (3½oz) plain Greek yoghurt
3 tablespoons seeded mustard
2 tablespoons honey
salt and pepper

Method

Preheat oven to 200°C/400°F. Place chicken breasts between two sheets of baking paper and hammer with a mallet or rolling pin until evenly flattened. Cut into finger-width pieces, discarding any fat. Smash nuts with a pestle and mortar (or in a ziplock bag, smash with a mallet or rolling pin) until finely crushed. Set up three small bowls. Mix nuts, breadcrumbs, herbs and cheese in the first. Lightly beat egg in the second. Place flour in the third. Line a baking tray with baking paper. Roll a chicken piece in the flour until thinly coated and shake off any excess; then dip it in the egg and make sure it's evenly covered. Finally, roll it in the breadcrumb mix until fully coated and place carefully on the baking tray. Continue until all the chicken pieces have been encrusted. Lightly drizzle or spray light oil onto each tender.

Place baking tray in the oven and cook for 20 minutes, turning once. The chicken tenders should be crispy and bronzed on the outside and succulent on the inside when fully cooked.

Dipping sauce

While the tenders are cooking, mix all the dipping sauce ingredients together. Drizzle a swirl of honey on the top of the sauce. Serve at room temperature.

Pairing

This is a pairing that needs to be considered carefully because the seasoning of the crust is the dominant flavour, as opposed to the chicken. Prosecco has a nutty profile, with a crispy finish and lingering soft aftertaste that complements the nuttiness of the crust and also cleanses the oiliness nicely. The mustard in the dip adds a zingy flavour which is also counterbalanced by the crusty coating. An interesting combination.

Suggested match

Brut prosecco

PAIRING STYLE / COMPLEMENTING

APPLE & PEAR PARFAIT

with almonds, caramel & cinnamon

Is it a breakfast treat or a dessert? This one is definitely a dessert. With delicious layers of texture and flavour, the sensation is very enticing. This dessert could easily give the visual impression that it is rich and heavy and that it might leave you needing to sleep it off, but in fact it's surprisingly light and easy to consume – almost a guiltless pleasure.

Prep 15 min
Cook 20 min
Yield 2 large or 4 medium serves

Ingredients

- 100g (3½oz) whole or pre-crushed almonds
- 4 medium sweet apples, peeled and diced
- 2 pears, peeled and diced
- 2 tablespoons brown sugar
- ½ teaspoon cinnamon
- 1 heaped tablespoon butter/ olive spread
- 500g (1lb 2oz) plain Greek yoghurt
- vanilla essence
- 500g (1lb 2oz) tube of 'ice-cream topping' caramel sauce

Method

Preheat oven to 200°C/400°F. Crush the almonds and toast lightly in the oven and set to one side. Spread the peeled and diced fruit out on a foil-lined baking tray and brush lightly with oil. Mix brown sugar and cinnamon in a small bowl, and sprinkle it over fruit. Flip fruit and repeat on the opposite side. Bake for 20 minutes or until fruit has browned and tenderised. Transfer to a bowl. In a small saucepan, or a microwave, melt the butter and pour over the fruit. Mix carefully until fruit is fully coated.

Place the yoghurt in another bowl. Add ten drops of vanilla essence and mix until smooth. Set up your preferred number of glasses and put a layer of fruit on the bottom and a layer of caramel on top. Follow with a layer of crushed nuts and then a layer of yoghurt. Repeat the series of layers until you reach the top of the glass and finish with a caramel layer. Top with a dollop of yoghurt, a squeeze of caramel and sprinkle with nuts. Finally, dust with cinnamon. Serve immediately or refrigerate until you are ready to eat.

Pairing

This is a delicious pairing. The overall nuttiness along with the apple and pear flavours in the dessert are also key virtues that you will find in an Italian prosecco. The dessert looks rich and heavy but, surprisingly, the combination of caramel and yoghurt is delicately sweet, soft, creamy and more-ish, and the prosecco adds to the freshness.

Suggested match
Dry non-vintage prosecco ideally from Veneto, Italy

PAIRING STYLE / ENHANCING

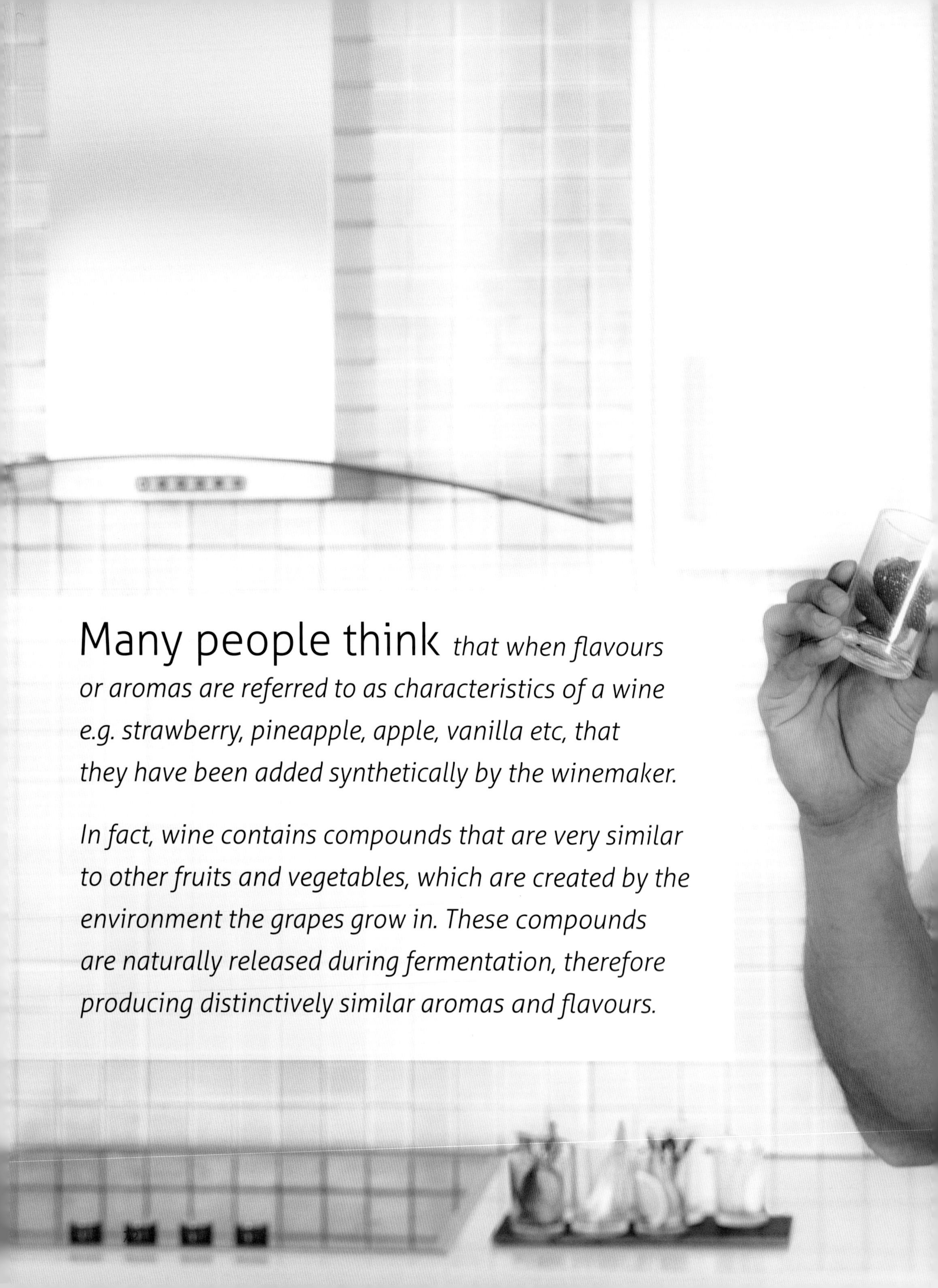

Many people think *that when flavours or aromas are referred to as characteristics of a wine e.g. strawberry, pineapple, apple, vanilla etc, that they have been added synthetically by the winemaker.*

In fact, wine contains compounds that are very similar to other fruits and vegetables, which are created by the environment the grapes grow in. These compounds are naturally released during fermentation, therefore producing distinctively similar aromas and flavours.

new world sparklings

NEW WORLD SPARKLINGS

'New World' is a term used to encompass a group of countries that were developed predominantly by immigrants from very established European winemaking countries from early in the 19th century. New World countries include Argentina, Australia, Chile, New Zealand and the US. More recent additions to the New World include the UK, India and China among others. South Africa is also sometimes referred to as a New World country, however, it was actually planted in advance of New World locations.

All New World countries have one very important common denominator that favours sparkling wine production: cool climate zones. In each territory there is a predominance of sparkling wine production in a cool climate area most conducive to ideal conditions for the best results. These are:

Argentina – Mendoza; *Australia* – Tasmania; *Chile* – Casablanca; *New Zealand* – Marlborough; *the US* – Sonoma Coast, California.

There is sometimes a dismissive perception that wine from some of these locations could be regarded as 'cheap and cheerful', however many very high quality representations also exist. It is definitely worthwhile to try for yourself without preconceived notions.

Several major French champagne houses have actually set up separate projects in New World countries, producing sparkling wines. In contrast to the strict rules and regulations for viticulture and production in Champagne, in New World countries there are no strict requirements to adhere to. This allows scope for experimentation. However, the reality is that most producers are attempting to create something as close to champagne as possible, therefore the traditional method of production is very popular, followed by charmat.

There is a diversity of grapes used for sparkling wine production in New World locations. Having said that, often traditional grapes (similar to those used in champagne e.g. chardonnay, pinot noir) are mainly utilised as the base juice for the wine.

Pairing New World sparkling wines

With fruity aromas and flavours, New World sparkling is usually fruitier than champagne and it often exhibits a taste reminiscent of pineapple ice-cream with a citric edge. The biscuity characteristic that is often found in champagne is not as pronounced in New World sparkling.

When pairing, the majority of New World sparkling will match effectively with similar dishes to champagne pairing (page 35), i.e. many cheeses, seafood, eggs, shellfish, pasta, light poultry, etc.

New World sparkling can be categorised as non-vintage, vintage and blanc de blancs (vintage or non-vintage) or blanc de noirs. As with champagne, vintage examples of New World sparkling can handle stronger flavours and richness. However, rich meats such as duck and pork match better with champagne.

1 Charmat ta
2 Tending the vi
3 Wine festival, Menc
4 Marlborough viney
5 Sonoma Coast, Califo
6 Vineyard, Son
Coast, Califo
7 Vineyards, Elqui Valley, C
8 Chardonnay grape crus
9 Argentinean barbe
10 New Zealand sh
11 Painted cliffs, Tasm

All photos © Shutters

New World
SPARKLING

QUICK REFERENCE

LOCATIONS
Argentina – Mendoza
Australia – Tasmania
Chile – Casablanca
New Zealand – Marlborough
US – California

GRAPES
Varied. Usually a base of chardonnay/pinot noir, plus options of chenin blanc, malbec, meunier, pinot grigio, riesling or sauvignon blanc, among others.

REGULATIONS
No defined regulations

WINEMAKING METHOD
All methods can be used but traditional method is the most popular.

ACIDITY Varied

ALCOHOL 11–12%

IDEAL PAIRING
Similar dishes to champagne pairing, ideally the lighter options like salad, seafood, pasta, etc

cheese *match*

Fondue is something that I associate with childhood when my parents had dinner parties, but it's definitely time for a revival! It's a great party starter that will inevitably stir some fond memories. Even better, fondue sets are relatively easy to find in thrift shops as well as homewares stores. If you're stuck, a (very clean) incense burner can do the job. A three-cheese combination of gruyère, cheddar and emmental is the most popular. You can dip whatever you fancy.

Suggested match

New World sparklings can match really well with these warm cheesy flavours, refreshing the palate, and complementing the creamy, oily tones. Aim for a vintage option if available, for a most effective counterbalance to the strength of cheese flavours.

Ingredients

200g (7oz) gruyère cheese, grated

200g (7oz) mild cheddar cheese, grated

200g (7oz) emmental cheese, grated

1 tablespoon plain (all-purpose) flour

1 cup (250ml/8½fl oz) lightly flavoured dry white wine

1 tablespoon lemon juice

a garlic clove to rub on the inside of the fondue bowl (optional)

bonus recipe

CHEESE FONDUE WITH DIPPERS

Method

This should be made just before you are ready to serve it. Prepare your dippers first. We have made a few suggestions but you can dip anything you'd like.

In a bowl, toss the cheeses together with the flour. Put a saucepan on a low heat and slowly bring the wine and lemon juice to a gentle simmer. Add the cheese very gradually, waiting until the last handful has melted before introducing another. Make sure it doesn't reach a boil. When all the cheese is melted and has reached a smooth consistency, you are ready to transfer it to your fondue pot.

Serving Keep the cheese warming in the fondue pot while you are dipping. Refresh your palate between mouthfuls with your chilled New World sparkling wine.

Dippers

bread sticks wrapped in finely sliced prosciutto*

salami cubes, toasted

crusty bread cubes, toasted

cauliflower trees, lightly boiled

Prep 20 min

Serves 4–6

**Note: The wrapped prosciutto will make the bread sticks go soft quickly, so only prepare immediately before serving*

TAGLIATELLE MARINARA
with light cream sauce & chives

This is a beautiful luxurious delicate pasta dish that won't leave you feeling overfull. It's important to keep the sauce of this recipe light and creamy in texture, so that it doesn't overwhelm the wine. The tagliatelle is effective at holding the sauce and wrapping it around the seafood as you eat. Many fish shops sell a pre-prepared marinara mix. For freshness of flavour the fish should be bought the same day as you intend to cook.

Prep 15 min
Cook 10 min
Serves 4

Ingredients

1 packet fresh tagliatelle pasta
2 heaped tablespoons of butter
1 garlic clove, finely chopped
3 spring onions (scallions), chopped
1/2 cup (125ml/4fl oz) dry white wine
200ml (7fl oz) cream
125g (4.5oz) double cream brie, chopped
1½ heaped tablespoons seeded mustard
400g (14oz) seafood marinara mix
bunch fresh chives, chopped

Method

Boil the tagliatelle as per packet's instructions and set to one side.

Over a high heat melt the butter and add the garlic. Once it starts to sizzle add the spring onions. Reduce heat slightly and stir regularly for about a minute. Add wine and allow to simmer for about 3–4 minutes until the liquid reduces by about a third. Add cream, brie and mustard. Continue to simmer and stir until all the cheese is dissolved.

Introduce the seafood and cook for a further 3–5 minutes, stirring continuously, until the seafood is ready to serve. Taste test to check that the seafood is tender.

Transfer to a large serving bowl and sprinkle liberally with fresh chives. In a colander, refresh the tagliatelle by pouring some hot water over it and shake out any excess water. Plate the tagliatelle and use a ladle to spoon the seafood and sauce on top. Garnish with a final sprinkle of chives.

Pairing

I've always been a fan of creamy seafood pastas. I recommend a fresh, citric New World sparkling to meld with the pasta flavours. The chives and spring onion create the link between the pasta and the wine, adding a fresh touch to the creaminess of the dish. For an extra-sensory challenge, explore the individual interactions the sparkling has with each of the different seafood elements. You will definitely feel fully satisfied after this meal.

Suggested match

NV New World sparkling, ideally a fresh young wine.

PAIRING STYLE / CLEANSING

MINI CHICKEN EMPANADAS
with three cheeses & spring onion

Empanadas are one of the fondest food memories I have from my first visit to Chile with David. Empanadas are even more of an institution in Chile than a pie is for Australians. A wide variety of fillings are available with a meat mixture, 'pino', being the most popular. However, our recipe is a less typical melt-in-the-mouth three-cheese and onion combo. Mini empanadas are great because they are ideal finger food for when you're entertaining and they are also filling.

Prep 1 hr

Cook 20 min

Yield 20–25 mini empanadas

Ingredients

2 large chicken breasts, diced

1 garlic clove, finely chopped

1 egg

150g (5½oz) light cheddar, grated

150g (5½oz) light Swiss cheese, grated

250g (9oz) cream cheese

4 spring onions (scallions), very finely sliced

2 tablespoons fresh basil, chopped

salt and pepper, to taste

sprinkle of chilli flakes (optional)

1 packet of puff pastry, defrosted

Method

Preheat oven to 180°C/350°F. Over a medium heat, start frying the chicken and garlic in a medium frying pan. Cover the chicken with a large saucepan lid on an angle (you can use a wooden spoon to achieve this) and add a small splash of water to retain humidity and promote juiciness in the chicken. Cook until tender and ready to eat.

Whisk the egg in a small bowl. Set aside. In a large bowl, combine the cooked chicken, grated cheeses, cream cheese, onions, basil and chilli flakes and mix together. Season with salt and pepper. Place the pastry on a floured work surface and cut out approximately 16cm (6¼ inches) diameter circles (we used a saucer as a cutting guide). Spoon a heaped teaspoon of the filling into the middle of each circle, being careful not to overfill. Brush the edges with the egg wash and fold each circle in half. Gently press on the top of the empanada to release any air.

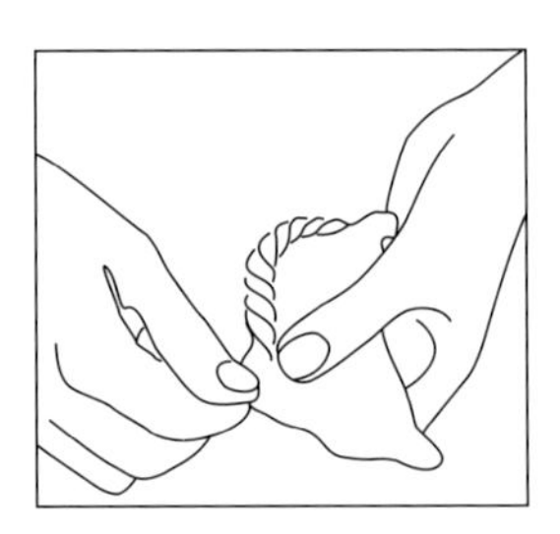

Fig. 2. Repulgue method. Pinch the pastry together, pull it out slightly and then fold it back onto itself.

Sealing You can simply press the edges together with a fork, however for the authentic finish we used the repulgue technique – it's easier than you might think – see Fig. 2. Squeeze the edges together with your fingers. Then it's a simple pinch and fold process. Starting from one corner, pinch a finger-width together and pull it out gently and then fold it over onto itself. Move another finger-width away and do the same, but fold a slight overlap onto the first fold. Continue until you reach the other side. Brush the top with some egg. Bake until golden brown, about 20 minutes.

Pairing

This is a creative take on a classic Chilean favourite. The flaky baked pastry yields to the rich textural sensation of the three cheeses enveloping the chicken. The spring onion creates a link between the melted cheese stretch and the crisp essence of the wine. A non-vintage sparkling effectively cleanses the palate of the rich flavours, with a fresh fizz to prepare for the second bite.

Suggested match

Non-vintage New World sparkling

PAIRING STYLE / CLEANSING

SHORTBREAD COOKIES
with macadamia nuts

The whole house smells gorgeous after baking these cookies. This is an excellent 'feet up with a book' pleasure, ideally in a hammock. It's such a magic moment to be lying comfortably, favourite music in the background, gently rocking, with a quality vintage sparkling tingling on your tongue and the butteriness of the cookies and wine melding into a lush blend of perfection – pure heaven.

Prep 15 min
Cook 20 min
Yield 14–18 cookies depending on cut size

Ingredients

2⅓ cups (300g/10½oz) plain (all-purpose) flour, sifted

250g (9oz) butter, softened

⅔ cup (150g/5½oz) caster (superfine) sugar

1 teaspoon vanilla essence

large handful macadamia nuts, roughly chopped

Method

Preheat oven to 160°C/320°F. Line two baking trays with baking paper. Place flour in a large bowl and slowly add butter, sugar and vanilla, mixing with a fork until it reaches a smooth texture. Add macadamia nuts and continue to mix until evenly distributed.

Divide dough into two portions. With a rolling pin, roll one portion between two sheets of baking paper until approximately 6mm (¼ inch) thick. Remove top layer of baking paper and cut dough into shapes using a cookie cutter. Reform the waste dough and continue to cut until all used. Repeat with the second portion. Transfer cookies to baking trays, leaving at least a finger-width space between each. Prick the top of each cookie with a fork. Bake for 20 minutes or until golden, swapping the trays halfway through cooking. Cool until firm, dust with icing sugar and serve.

Pairing

A vintage New World sparkling will often express buttery, nutty and biscuity characteristics. Shortbread is a classic buttery, crunchy biscuit. The addition of macadamias adds a delectable nutty element. Vanilla is the finishing touch to complete the perfect link between these two delightful indulgences. It's almost impossible not to keep reaching for the biscuits as long as your glass is charged.

Suggested match

New World sparkling, ideally vintage

PAIRING STYLE / COMPLEMENTING

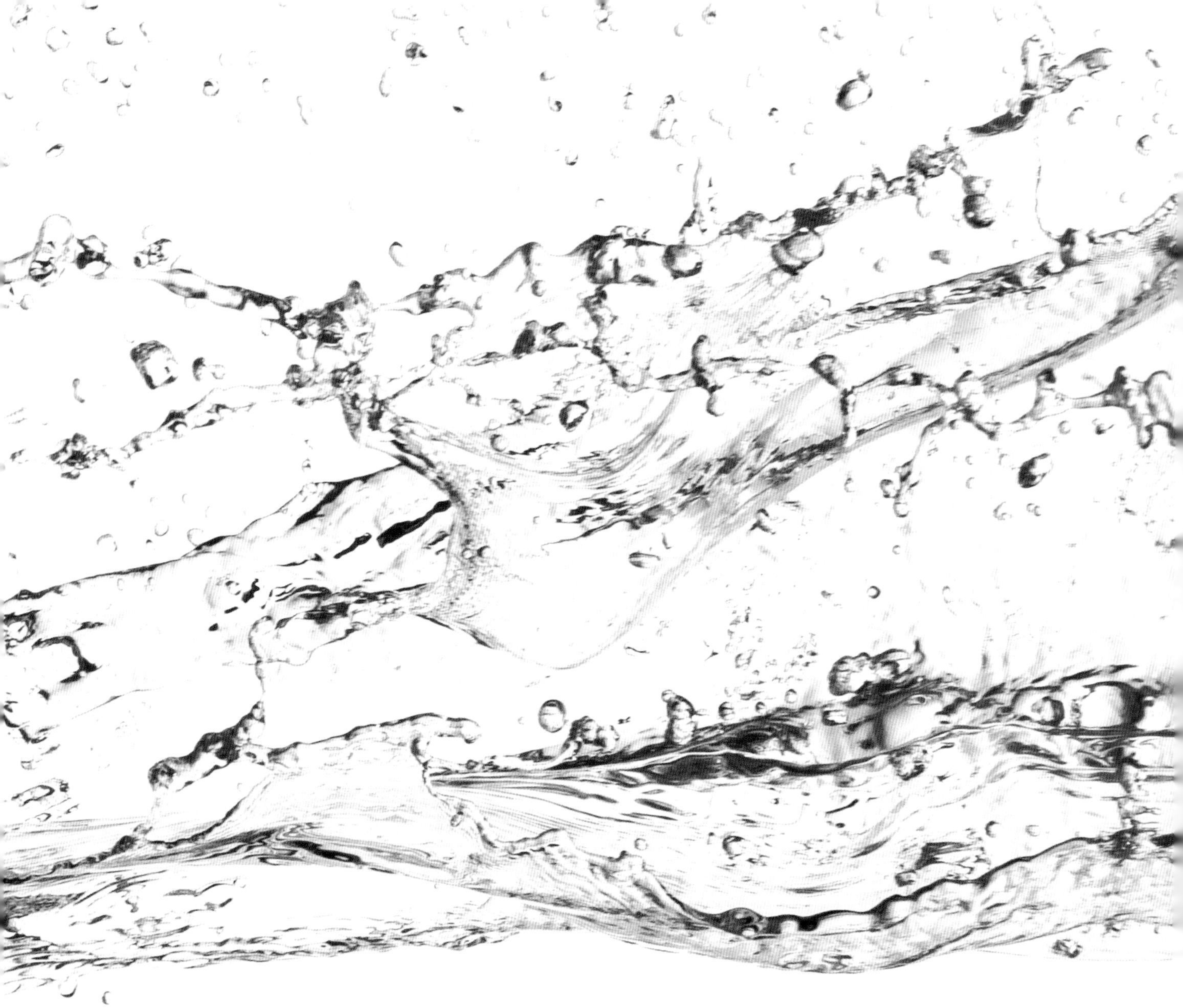

When visiting a non-specialist outlet to buy wine, *it can be surprising how often the staff are unaware of the correct name for different varieties of sparkling wine. For example, if you receive a blank response upon asking for cava or prosecco, try requesting Spanish or Italian sparkling wine instead. You'll often see a light bulb moment!*

sparkling rosé

SPARKLING ROSÉ

Rosé wine is not a grape or a region, it's a genre, like white or red wine. It is distinctive for its pink or peachy colour. Rosé is produced in non-sparkling as well as sparkling formats, and food pairing suggestions will generally suit both. Sparkling rosé was initially inspired by rosé champagne (also known as pink champagne), the first of which was produced around the late 17th century.

It was the Portuguese, however, who revolutionised sparkling rosé's popularity, with two slightly sweet, lightly sparkling examples, Mateus and Lancers, after World War II. So influential were these wines that they dominated the segment for quite some time and in the 1970s they were the most popular wines in the world. Eventually, particularly in recent years, a preference for a drier style has emerged and these once dominant wines are no longer as popular.

While sparkling rosé is made in nearly all sparkling wine producing countries, champagne rosé and French rosé from the Loire, Provence and Rhone regions would probably be the most well-known. Other countries producing sparkling rosé very worthy of consideration include Italy (rosato), Germany, Spain (rosado) and Portugal (rosado), along with New World countries Argentina, Australia, Chile, New Zealand and the US.

Making sparkling rosé

Rosé wines get their colour from red wine grapes, although white wine, usually chardonnay, is often found in the blend. When grapes are pressed, regardless of whether they are white or red grapes, the resulting juice is usually a clear white wine colour. There are three methods to create rosé. Often some non-sparkling red wine, usually pinot noir, is also added to the blend, to manipulate the colour and flavour. Otherwise the colour is created by leaving the red grape skins to sit in the juice for a period of time, which facilitates the pigment from the skin to slowly bleed into the juice. The type of grapes used and the duration that the skins are in contact with the juice will define the resulting colour and influence the flavour. A third method, called saignée, uses some juice removed from the production of a red wine.

Almost any grape can be used to make a non-sparkling rosé, but with sparkling rosé, chardonnay, pinot noir and meunier are most popular. This is likely because these are the same grape varieties used in champagne, as well as champagne rosé.

Pairing sparkling rosé

Other than vintage champagne rosé, sparkling rosé wines are generally designed to be enjoyed fresh and soon. This is not a style intended for cellaring. Most rosés are expected to be consumed within two to three years.

Sparkling rosé is a very versatile wine for pairing. While it is usually pink or peach in colour, it's important not to confuse it with the other pink-coloured sparkling style, moscato, which is always very sweet. Sparkling rosé is available in a broad range of styles and it is usually distinctively dry. It can range from light and delicate to quite concentrated in flavour, depending on the grapes and the blend. It has a particular affinity with charcuterie (cured and smoked meats), duck, shellfish, berries and chocolate but you can experiment freely with cheeses, egg and pasta dishes, as well as salad, and most light meats.

1 Bakery, Provence, Fra
2 Tending the v
3 Coastal woodland, Tasm
4 River Douro, Port
5 Lavendar, Provence, Fra
6 Chateau de Sau
Loire Valley, Fra
7 Peille, Provence, Fra
All photos ©Shutters

8 Grape harvest, Port
© *Marafona/Shutters*

9 Nice, Fra
© *marekusz/Shutters*

10 Wine glass bay, Tasm
© *Shutters*

SPARKLING ROSÉ

QUICK REFERENCE

LOCATION
All sparkling wine producing countries

GRAPES
Chardonnay, pinot noir, meunier and, less often, a broad variety of other grapes.

REGULATIONS
Regionally dependent

WINEMAKING METHOD
All methods can be used

ACIDITY Varied

ALCOHOL 11–12.5%

IDEAL PAIRING
Sparkling rosé is a very versatile option and pairs particularly well with cured meats, shellfish, salads, desserts and chocolate.

cheese *match*

Queso fresco, simply meaning 'fresh cheese', is a favourite in Spain and many countries in Latin America. It is a light, moist, fresh, mild, creamy cheese that can complement everything from salad to savoury dishes. A light creamy fetta can be used as a substitute. Soaking the fetta in water for a short while will reduce the saltiness if you find it too much.

This pairing suggestion, which unites sparkling rosé with watermelon and mint, should excite your taste buds with the unfamiliar combination of sensations.

Watermelon is usually a tricky fruit to wine pair, but the versatility of sparkling rosé is more than a match. The combination of creamy, spicy cheese with the refreshing watermelon and mint, united with the fruity flavour of the sparkling rosé, is sensational.

Ingredients

500g (1lb 2oz) queso fresco or smooth fetta

1 garlic clove, roasted until soft

1 small fresh chilli, seeded and finely diced

1 tablespoon lemon juice

2 tablespoons olive oil

6 tablespoons fresh mint, destemmed and finely chopped

½ watermelon

Method

Use a blending stick or blender to mix the cheese, garlic, chilli, lemon juice, olive oil and mint (reserve some additional mint for serving). Process until smooth.

bonus recipe

WATERMELON WITH MINT HERB CREAM CHEESE

Serving

Serve with dipping sticks of chilled fresh watermelon sprinkled with finely chopped mint. Use a small spoon to smear the watermelon with the dip.

CHARCUTERIE

There's charcuterie and then there's *charcuterie*. I didn't fully appreciate the difference until I had the pleasure of enjoying a magnificent charcuterie at a five-star restaurant that David once worked for. You really can taste quality. So while putting together a charcuterie may seem like a simple undertaking, it's taking the time to source the best ingredients that will leave your guests discussing it all night.

Prep 10 min
Serves 4–6

Suggested ingredients

prosciutto
salami
pâté terrine
olives
gherkins
bread sticks
crispy french bread

Method

There are key elements to a great charcuterie that will balance the flavours and create interest and pleasing contrasts. The word *charcuterie* is French in origin, and refers to a delicatessen-style shop that usually sells a broad variety of quality meats and meat-based products.

Meats Meat is the centrepiece of a good charcuterie. A variety of dried, smoked and cured meats are an ideal combination. Thin slicing is key for softer textured meats, whereas chunky slicing of firmer meats, such as salami, works well. Meats can include prosciutto, jamón serrano, pepperoni, Spanish salami, soppressata and many other salamis and cured meats.

Accompaniments Pâtés and terrines are usually meat-based and a lovely complement to the meat selection. Pickles are a great acidic contrast to meat. Options like olives (stuffed, marinated or plain), pickled onions, gherkins, chutney and other marinated or pickled produce are essential. Mediterranean olive oil and some dukkah for dipping the bread is also a nice touch. Chilli, mustard and other sauces are also welcome flavours.

Bread A range of bread options will complete your selection nicely. Aim to include some crackers or water biscuits, a doughy bread such as French stick (baguette) or sourdough, and something crunchy like bread sticks.

Invite everyone to eat directly from the board or offer small side plates if it's a larger group.

Pairing

This food and wine pairing has many angles due to the different levels of salt, oil and texture in the charcuterie. The sparkling rosé has a complementary fresh strawberry character as well as a dry lingering finish. Explore the interaction of the fresh, crisp and fruity sparkling rosé with every element of the charcuterie. You will be surprised at how quickly you can consume the lot, as the wine really accelerates the experience.

Suggested match
New World
dry sparkling rosé

PAIRING STYLE / COUNTERBALANCE

SPANISH SALAMI NOODLES

with fetta, pinenuts & lettuce

Sometimes a great blend of flavours can be an accidental discovery. Such was the case when I planned to create a spaghetti dish and discovered I only had noodles. Surprisingly the noodles add a whole different dimension that is really appetising, but of course you could always make this with spaghetti if you would prefer. Leaving the addition of the lettuce until just before serving is important, because the crispy texture is a great feature.

Prep 20 min
Cook 10 min
Serves 4

Ingredients

400g (14oz) fresh fried chow mein noodles
30g (1oz) pine nuts
½ small sweet gem or cos (romaine) lettuce
50g (1¾oz) Spanish salami, cut into thin, short strips
100g (3½oz) soft smooth fetta, diced
extra virgin olive oil
salt and pepper

Method

Boil noodles according to instructions on the packet and put to one side. Toast pine nuts on a tray in the oven at a medium heat until they are lightly browned. Cut the lettuce into fine ribbons.

Place the noodles in a large bowl and sprinkle all the other ingredients on top. Mix together using a spaghetti serving spoon. Drizzle generously with olive oil. Add salt and pepper to taste. Mix again and then serve.

Pairing

The salami, fetta, pine nuts and olive oil combination will cover your palate, coating your mouth with a pleasant savoury, creamy texture. The sparkling rosé adds freshness and cleanses the palate superbly. The dry savoury finish works in harmony, in particular with the salami and pine nuts. There's a nice lasting finish created by the combination of the fetta and the mousse of the wine.

Suggested match

Sparkling rosé, ideally vintage

PAIRING STYLE / CLEANSING

SUSHI SALAD
with smoked salmon

This recipe is top of my favourites list. I have always been a big fan of Japanese food, and creating a salad that utilises a lot of the elements that you can often find at a sushi bar was fun. It is an ideal starter, but it also has enough substance to stand alone, or be served as an exciting side. Part of the pleasure of putting this dish together is a trip to the Asian supermarket to source some of the elements. I was delighted to also discover that edamame beans can often be found in the frozen section of many supermarkets.

Prep 20 min

Serves 4 as a lunch salad or 6 as a starter

Ingredients

1 small Chinese cabbage, shredded

1 gem (baby cos/romaine) lettuce, shredded

1 avocado, sliced in thin pieces

200g (7oz) smoked salmon, cut into pieces

1 packet onion sprouts

200g (7oz) edamame beans, boiled and shelled

1 packet crispy noodles

3 tablespoons tobiko (flying fish roe) caviar

1 small packet roasted (or toasted) nori (seaweed), cut into thin ribbons

sprigs of dill, to serve

Dressing

160ml (5.5fl oz) peanut oil

2 tablespoons soy sauce

3 tablespoons lemon juice

Method

In the bowl(s) you intend to serve the salad start by creating a bed of Chinese cabbage and gem lettuce. Gradually build up the rest of the salad in layers in the following order: avocado, salmon, onion sprouts, edamame, crispy noodles, tobiko caviar and, finally, the nori ribbons. Finish by adding some extra onion sprouts, salmon, crispy noodles and edamame on top. Refrigerate until ready to serve.

Mix all the elements of the dressing together and shake well. Pour over salad when ready to serve. Finally, top with some sprigs of dill.

For an alternative serving idea, you can wrap the salad in rice paper to make fresh rice paper rolls. It also presents really well individually served in large glass tumblers.

Pairing

The combination of textures is outstanding. The crispy noodles and crunchy caviar, cabbage and lettuce contrast beautifully with the tenderness of the salmon and creaminess of the avocado and edamame. The refreshing aromatic characteristics of sparkling rosé work in synergy with the varying textures and intensities of flavour, resulting in a pleasant sensation in every mouthful.

Suggested match

Sparkling rosé, ideally pinot noir dominant

PAIRING STYLE / ENHANCING

All wines are better when they are older, right?

Wrong, all wines have a life span and, in fact, the majority are designed to be consumed in a relatively short space of time. There are only a small percentage of wines that are intended to survive into old age. In the case of sparkling wines, generally speaking cellarable wines are of high pedigree and therefore in a high price bracket – particularly vintage champagnes.

Fluffy scrambled eggs
with mango salsa 108

Shrimp, almond &
pomegranate salad 110

Moscato cream cakelets with
raspberry coulis & pastry fingers 112

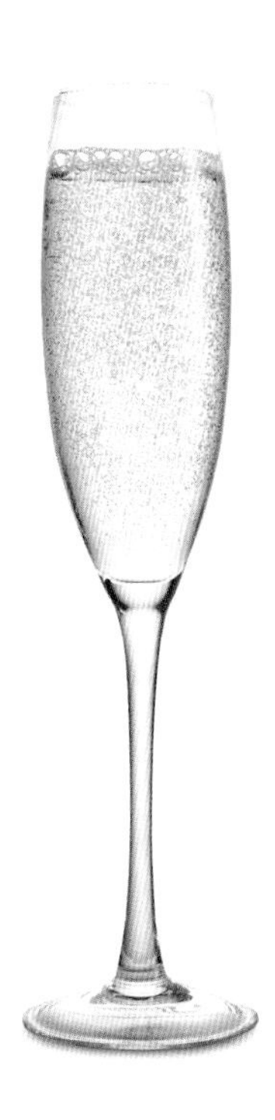

moscato

MOSCATO

Sparkling moscato originated in Piedmont in Italy hundreds of years ago. Here it is called Moscato d'Asti; Asti being the name of a province of Piedmont, close to Turin. Moscato d'Asti is produced under careful regulation. Moscato is a lightly sparkling, low alcohol sweet wine traditionally derived from the muscat grape. It can be white in colour, or pink due to the addition of (usually) a small amount of merlot. Originally winemakers produced this wine for their own lunchtime consumption. Being light in style and low in alcohol meant they could continue working in the afternoon. Mass production of moscato began at the end of the 19th century.

Moscato-style wine is also produced all around the world without regulation and can vary, but the underlying format of sweetness with low alcohol is usually reasonably consistent.

Blend
Moscato is produced using the charmat method and is designed to be consumed fresh and young. It is currently enjoying a phase of significant popularity, particularly in the US, and sales have been increasing consistently since 2011.

Pairing moscato
Moscato is often considered to be a dessert wine, so it is ideally paired with sweet dishes, desserts, ice-cream and treats. It usually has a yummy Turkish delight flavour and often smells like sweet talc or perfume. It also works well as an aperitif, or as a refreshing burst of sweetness with a light savoury dish, especially on a sunny day.

Main im
Langhe, Asti, Piedmont, I
© Shutters

L
Orta San Gi
Asti, Piedmont, I
© Shutters

Palio di Asti fest
© Fa

Lake Orta, Piedmont,
© Shutters

Turin, Piedmont,
© Stefano En
Shutters

Barolo Castello di La V
Piedmont,
© Shutters

MOSCATO D'ASTI

QUICK REFERENCE

LOCATION
Asti, Piedmont, Italy

GRAPES
Muscat

REGULATIONS
Strict viticulture and production requirements

WINEMAKING METHOD
Charmat method

ACIDITY Low–medium

ALCOHOL Usually 5–5.5%

IDEAL PAIRING
Moscato is quite different to other sparkling wines in that it is usually very sweet and low in alcohol. It is mainly suited for aperitif or desserts and lovely with soft cheeses, ice-cream, and sweet treats as well as light savoury dishes or salad.

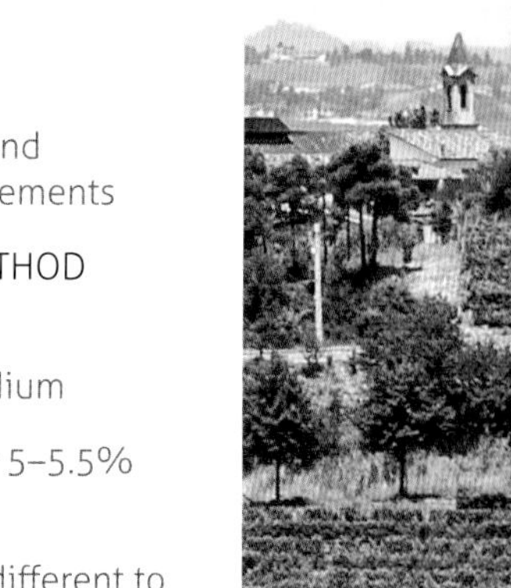

cheese *match*

Moscato offers an attractive sweetness that is often presented alongside dessert. In this case we have combined cheese with sweet elements that can offer a sweet ending to a meal, without being a dessert as such.

Add sliced strawberry to quince paste and triple cream brie on wafer or lavosh biscuits and you have created a heavenly sweet cheese experience. The moscato accentuates the flavours of the strawberries and quince paste in this complementary pairing.

FLUFFY SCRAMBLED EGGS
with mango salsa

Scrambled eggs are a staple brunch favourite, but getting them just right is elusive for many. Most cooks have their own special techniques. This is our tried and tested method after many years of Sunday brunches. The mango salsa adds something special to the experience and creates an edge that can make it an appealing option for lunch as well as a breakfast or brunch.

Prep 10 min
Cook 5 min
Serves 2

Salsa ingredients

1 cup (125g/4½oz) fresh mango, diced

½ cucumber, seeded and diced

1 tomato, finely diced

3 tablespoons fresh lime juice

2 tablespoons fresh coriander (cilantro), finely chopped

1 tablespoon chives, chopped

salt and pepper, to taste

Scramble ingredients

2 large eggs per person

splash of milk

salt & pepper

To serve

crusty bread, sliced, toasted and buttered

Method

Salsa Use a blender/food processor to roughly mix the mangos with all the other salsa ingredients. Make sure not to purée the mixture – you should retain texture and colour in the salsa. Refrigerate until you are almost ready to serve, then return to room temperature.

Scramble Crack the eggs into a bowl. Add a generous splash of milk and mix on high with a stick blender for about 20 seconds. Season with salt and pepper and pour into a frying pan. Set the heat to high, and keep the mixture constantly moving with a soft spatula until it starts to form solids on the bottom. Reduce the heat slightly and gently push the solid forms off the bottom of the pan as they appear. Continue moving the mixture with the spatula until the eggs look almost how you would like them. Remove the eggs from the heat just before all the liquid has evaporated. The eggs will continue to cook for a minute or so after they have been removed from the heat.

Serve the eggs on toast with the salsa as a side, or over the top, depending on your preference. Garnish with fresh herbs and cracked pepper. Enjoy!

Pairing

Such an unexpected combination. The mango salsa is the star of this dish and it creates the link between the food and the sparkling moscato. At first I was a bit hesitant about the whole idea, but I was mightily impressed with the result. It is the perfect brunch, leaving a pleasant sweetness but without comprising on texture, volume or freshness.

Suggested match

Moscato

PAIRING STYLE / COMPLEMENTING

SHRIMP SALAD

with almonds & pomegranate

Discovering pomegranate as a salad addition was an Australian revelation for us. Luckily you can often find them pre-seeded in a convenience pack, but to seed them yourself here is a handy technique. First pierce the skin all the way around the diameter of the fruit, without cutting through. Then rip the fruit in half with your hands. Fill a large bowl with water, submerge one half and free the seeds from each chamber. You'll see the skin floats to the surface. Repeat with the other half. Remove skin and strain fruit, no mess!

Prep 20 min
Cook 10 min
Serves 4 small serves

Ingredients

½ cup (70g/2oz) slivered almonds
500g (1lb 2oz) small prawns (shrimp), cooked
4 tablespoons light olive oil
2 tablespoons fresh lime juice
salt and pepper, to taste
2 small cos (romaine) lettuce, washed
handful of small radishes, slivered
half a cucumber, seeded and ribboned with a potato peeler
1 pomegranate, seeded (approx. ¾ cup seeds/130g/4.5oz)

Method

Pre-heat the oven to 180°C/350°F. Place almond slivers on a sheet of baking paper on a flat tray and roast for 10 minutes or until browned, agitating occasionally. Set aside. Flash-fry the shrimp at a high heat with a tablespoon of olive oil to lightly coat the pan. You should only need a minute or two for each side. The shrimp is ready when it changes to an opaque consistency and starts to curl slightly. Put to one side.

Mix the remaining oil with the lime juice and salt and pepper. In a salad bowl set up a bed of lettuce and sprinkle the shrimp and radishes evenly. Distribute the cucumber ribbons on top and then sprinkle the pomegranate generously over everything. Finally, pour the oil dressing evenly over the top.

Serve in small bowls as a fresh starter, or as a side to a larger dish.

Pairing

Salads can sometimes be very one-dimensional, well, not this one! The key link between the food and wine is the pomegranate, which shares similar characteristics to the moscato but with a slightly tart finish. The shrimp gives the substance to hold all the crunchy, juicy flavours together. I often struggle to feel satisfied after a salad, in particular due to lack of flavour, but this salad is lovely and the moscato gives such a lift to the overall experience.

Suggested match
Moscato d'Asti

PAIRING STYLE / COMPLEMENTING

MOSCATO CREAM CAKELETS

with raspberry sauce & puff pastry fingers

This is lush, decadent indulgence at it's best. The moscato in the sponge adds something unexpected and gives a luxurious sensation to the cakelets. They are very easy to make and the final assembly has a satisfying artistry. Don't be surprised if your guests request seconds, ours did.

Prep 15 min
Cook 20 min
Yield 8 cakelets

Ingredients

¾ cup (170g/6oz) caster (superfine) sugar

2 eggs

½ cup (125ml/4fl oz) moscato

2 cups (300g/10½oz) self-raising flour, sifted

¾ cup (190ml/6½fl oz) milk

1 teaspoon vanilla essence

100g (3.5oz) fresh or frozen raspberries, washed and diced/ defrosted

Sauce & decorating

½ sheet puff pastry, thawed

200g (7oz) raspberries, washed and diced

½ cup (115g/4oz) caster (superfine) sugar

1¼ cups (300ml/10fl oz) thickened (whipping) cream

icing (confectioners') sugar, to decorate

Method

Cakes Pre-heat the oven to 180°C/350°F. Whisk the sugar, eggs, moscato, flour, milk and vanilla essence until you achieve a smooth, frothy texture. If the mixture is very thick you can add a little more wine. Fold in the raspberries and mix until evenly distributed. Pour into a lightly greased or lined muffin tray for 8 large muffins. Put to one side. Cut the puff pastry into several strips about a finger-width wide (two per cakelet) and place on a baking tray. Bake cakelets and puff pastry together for 20 minutes or until both are lightly golden. Remove from oven and cool on a wire tray.

Sauce Combine the raspberries and icing sugar in a saucepan. Add 50ml (1¾fl oz) of water. Stir over a low heat until the raspberries disintegrate and the sugar dissolves. Remove from heat. If you prefer, strain the sauce to remove the seeds.

Raspberry cream centre Slice the top off each cake, cut into quarters and set aside. Cut a hole out of the remaining bottom section and fill with raspberry sauce. Whip the cream until thick and pipe on top of the raspberry centre, covering the whole diameter.

Assembly Position the quarters of cakelet on angles on top of the cream layer. Top with more cream. Break two small pieces of puff pastry to size and press into the cream. Finally, on the serving plate, spoon the sauce all over the cake and lightly dust with icing sugar.

Pairing

With moscato as an ingredient in the sponge – drinking the soft, sweet bubble of a light moscato is the obvious accompaniment. Desserts can sometimes be overpowered by sweet wine, leaving only one flavour. The beauty here is that it is delicate and soft and the interaction of the Turkish delight and rose petal flavours of the wine give a pleasant, sophisticated finish.

Suggested match
A light sparkling moscato

PAIRING STYLE / PARALLELING

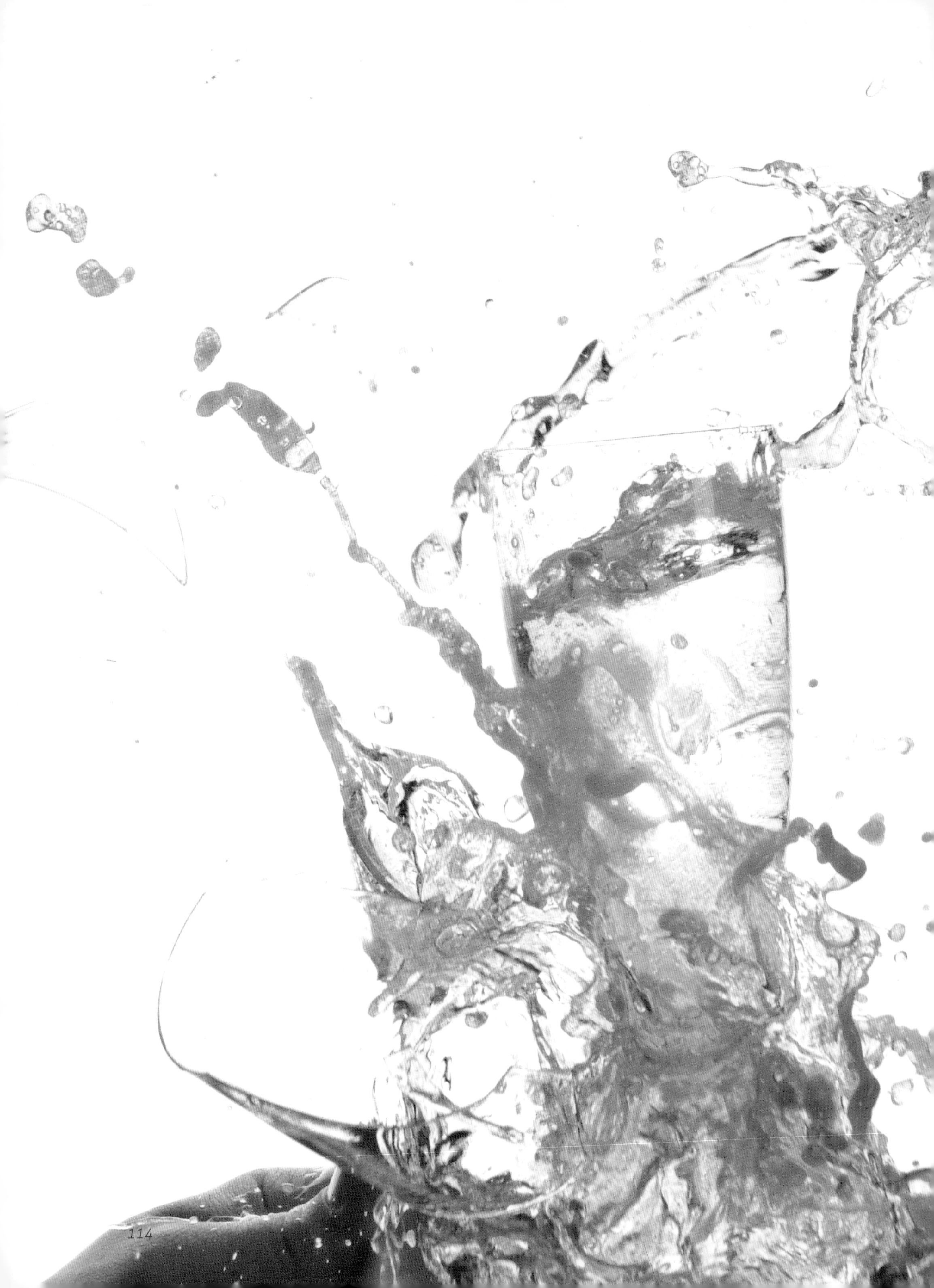

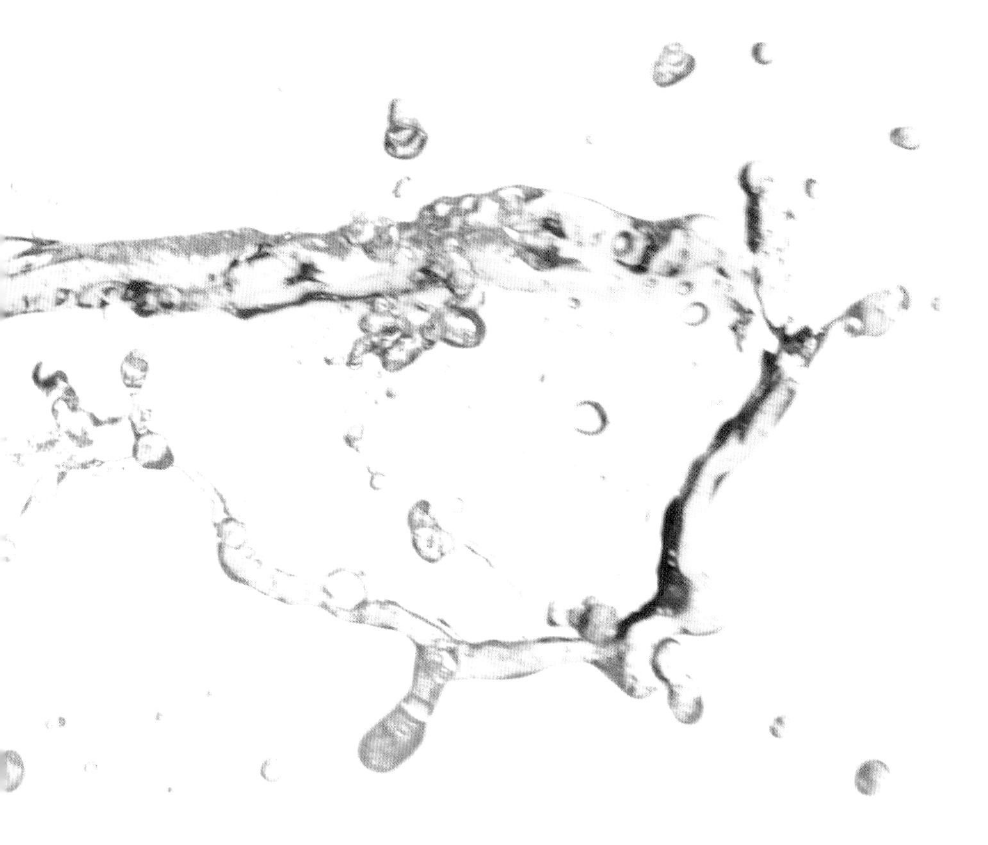

Does sparkling wine make you drunk more quickly than still wine?

Yes! Studies have concluded that drinking sparkling wine of the same alcohol level as a still wine will create a significantly higher blood alcohol level after a shorter period of time due to the CO_2 accelerating the speed of the alcohol's journey through the body.

Ref: 2001 Study at the University of Surrey, UK, lead by Dr Fran Ribout

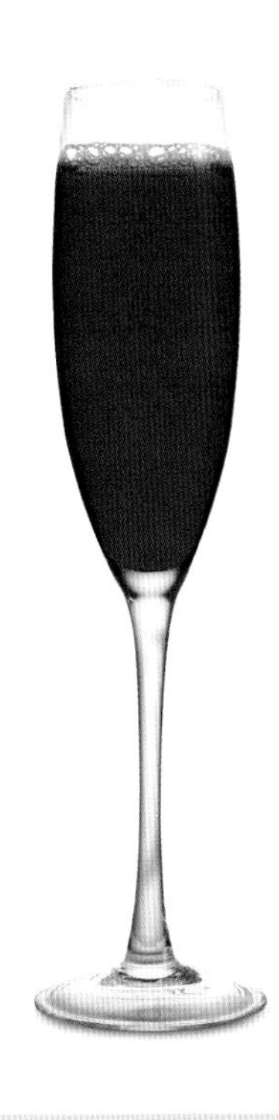

sparkling reds

SPARKLING REDS

Lambrusco from Italy and sparkling shiraz from Australia are the two styles of sparkling red that are presented here. There are other sparkling reds available, but these two are the main options that you will find easily. The majority of other sparkling reds are produced in Italy with relatively unusual grape varieties. Australian wineries also experiment with varieties such as merlot, pinot noir and cabernet sauvignon.

Lambrusco
Usually lightly sparkling (frizzante), lambrusco is designed to be drunk young and fresh. It has a reputation for being light, cheap and sweet. While this is true for a large proportion of lambrusco there are actually several styles available. Produced under regulation, there are eight sub-varieties of the lambrusco grape that are permitted in a blend. Four defined zones of winemaking in the Emilia-Romagna region vary the blend to produce their own style. This can vary from secco (dry), amabile (semi-sweet) to dolce (sweet). The drier, higher quality lambrusco is generally produced using the more laborious traditional method, whereas the sweeter, mass produced version is usually created under the charmat method.

When paired, this wine works with a cleansing style, cutting through fattiness with its acidity and aiding in the digestion of rich sauces and meats. It's a great accompaniment to Italian fare, such as pizza, salami and tomato-based sauces. Secco style works particularly well with local specialities such as balsamic vinegar, parmigiano-reggiano (parmesan cheese) and prosciutto ham. Amabile is an ideal companion of red fruits and desserts. Dolce can be a dessert in itself, or perhaps serve with a sugary treat.

Sparkling shiraz
In 1881, French winemaker Auguste D'Argent working in collaboration with a Melbourne doctor and owner of The Victorian Champagne Company, offered the inspiration to create the first sparkling reds in Australia. Initially it was referred to as 'sparkling burgundy' until French regulators demanded that wines produced outside of the Burgundy region should stop using the name. While this initial venture failed, soon after another Frenchman, Edmund Mazure, working in Adelaide, pioneered the use of shiraz grapes in sparkling red. Now produced predominantly in South Australia and the Great Western Region, Victoria, the wine is typically rich and complex with a frothy mousse.

Unlike lambrusco, good quality sparkling shiraz can be ideal for aging. Younger sparkling shiraz is refreshing, rich, fruity and juicy with a touch of sweetness. Older examples express additional savoury characteristics and the bubble is more delicate and refined. Most sparkling shiraz is blended with a small percentage of other grapes. These can include cabernet sauvignon, pinot noir and grenache, among others. As with lambrusco, the higher quality sparkling shiraz is generally produced using the traditional method, with bulk production relying on the charmat method.

The lush richness of sparkling shiraz accented with a hint of sweetness offers an ideal marriage with rich meat and gamey flavours, particularly with aged wines. As a result, duck, lamb, pork, kangaroo and venison are all perfect companions. Chocolate and berries are also great choices, and can work equally well with a younger wine.

1 Bologna, Emilia-Romagna,
2 Tending the v
3 San Leo castle, Ri
Emilia-Romagna,
4 Vineyard and ca
Emilia-Romagna,
5 Large wooden wine
6 Vineyard, Mclaren Vale, Aust
7 Emilia-Romagna,
8 Grape vines, McLaren
South Aust
9 Vineyard, Aust
10 Great Ocean Road, Aust

LAMBRUSCO

QUICK REFERENCE

LOCATION
Emilia-Romagna, Italy

GRAPES
The lambrusco grape and eight sub-varieties

REGULATIONS
Defined viticulture and production requirements

WINEMAKING METHOD
Traditional method
Charmat method

ACIDITY Low

ALCOHOL 11%+

IDEAL PAIRING
Salami and cured meats, tomato-based sauces and pizza, as well as red fruits and desserts

SPARKLING SHIRAZ

QUICK REFERENCE

LOCATION
South Australia and the Great Western Region, Victoria.

GRAPES
Shiraz is often blended with a small percentage of other grapes such as cabernet sauvignon, pinot noir, etc

REGULATIONS
No defined production requirements

WINEMAKING METHOD
Traditional method
Charmat method

ACIDITY Low

ALCOHOL 12–14%

IDEAL PAIRING
Rich gamey meats, red fruits and chocolate

cheese *match*

Blue cheese with sparkling shiraz or lambrusco

There is such variety in the category of blue cheese that a book could be written on it alone. Blue cheese acquired its name due to the veins of edible blue mould that fracture the cheese.

Blue cheese is available in many styles, textures and intensities from all around the world. Familiarising yourself with the most well-known options is a good place to start.

Roquefort, France

No rind, white, tangy, crumbly and slightly moist, with distinctive veins of greeny blue mould.

Gorgonzola, Italy

Young gorgonzola is creamy, flavoursome, salty, pungent and moist. As it ages it can become crumbly and drier.

Danablu/Danish Blue, Denmark

Edible rind, semi-soft and creamy, salty, tangy, and sharply flavoured, although often milder than other blues.

Blue Stilton, England

Slightly acidic and semi-firm when young, this cheese actually mellows and becomes softer with age. It has a crusty rind and cylindrical shape.

Australia also produces a variety of blue cheese, with Tasmania offering the broadest and most well-known range.

Serving Suggestion

Sherry or port with blue cheese would be a pretty typical pairing suggestion, or even a sweet moscato to counterbalance the tang of the blue veins, but an interesting option is pairing with a sparkling shiraz or lambrusco.

Both lambrusco and shiraz have an underlying sweetness that offers a nice counterbalance: the earthiness of the wine is accentuated, making it seem richer; plus the fruitiness of the wine enhances the tanginess of the cheese.

Try lambrusco with younger, blue cheese and sparkling shiraz with an aged blue. A simple addition of sliced pear complements this enhancing match.

BBQ LAMB CUTLETS

with mint & rosemary sauce

Every self-respecting Chilean male makes it his business to be king of the barbecue, and David is no exception. Culturally, the barbecue is an even more important social gathering in Chile than in Australia (which is really saying something). And you can forget a basic sausage sizzle or BYO, these guys only serve the best they can offer. In Chile the barbecue is the focal point for everyone (both genders) and meat is often served in bite-sized pieces on a wooden platter that is passed around as each item is ready.

Prep 5 min
Cook 20 min
Serves 4

Mint sauce

1 small bunch mint leaves, finely chopped

3 sprigs rosemary, stripped and finely chopped

2 teaspoons sugar

¼ cup (60ml/2fl oz) boiling water

½ cup (125ml/4fl oz) white wine

For the cutlets

12 lamb cutlets

salt and pepper

Method

Mint sauce Place mint in a measuring jug. Pour boiling water over the mint and rosemary and add sugar. Stir until the sugar dissolves. Add vinegar and stir again. Allow to steep and serve when cooled to a comfortable temperature.

Lamb cutlets There can be a significant difference in meat quality so buy your cutlets from the best butcher you can find in your area. You are looking for very bright red meat and very white fat, both indicators of freshness. Cooking time will depend on your barbeque and personal taste. These instructions should produce a medium to well-done result. Adjust the cooking time to suit your preferences.

Clean the barbecue carefully so that there is no residue from previous cooking. Heat the grill to the maximum setting to burn off any remaining fat. Salt the cutlets thoroughly. Reduce barbeque to a low heat and place cutlets onto the grate and cook very slowly for approximately eight minutes or until pink juices appear on the surface.

Turn cutlets to the other side and cook for a further eight minutes or until the second side matches the appearance of the first. Place the meat on higher shelf of barbecue to drain and switch off burners. Lower hood (if available) to retain heat or cover in foil. Serve immediately, drizzled with mint sauce.

Pairing

Lamb has a strong aroma and flavour so you need a wine that can handle that richness. Sparkling shiraz balances well with this flavoursome dish. The mint sauce introduces a dimension of sweetness, which in conjunction with the mousse from the sparkling red, produces a lingering creamy sensation.

Suggested match

Non-vintage sparkling shiraz

PAIRING STYLE / *COMPLEMENTING*

ROAST DUCK

with cherry sauce

I've always thought of cooking duck as an overly ambitious idea, but when we decided that it would be a great pairing for a sparkling red I pushed my preconceived notions to one side, and was pleasantly surprised with how easy it was to make a lovely crispy duck with mouthwatering juicy meat. The best part is that our guests were suitably impressed also. The cherry sauce is definitely the cherry on top! You might need to pre-book with your butcher to source whole ducks.

Prep 20 min

Cook 1½ hours

Serves 4

Cherry sauce

350g (12.5oz) jar of pitted cherries (use all the juice and the cherries)

2 tablespoons balsamic vinegar

1 tablespoon soy sauce

1 heaped teaspoon brown sugar

1 tablespoon plain (all-purpose) flour

3 sprigs of fresh rosemary

Duck ingredients

1kg (2lb 3oz) of duck per person (i.e. use 2 x 2kg ducks for four people)

coarse sea salt

Method

Cherry sauce In a bowl place the cherries, cherry juice, vinegar, soy sauce, sugar and flour and mix with a blending stick. Pour into a saucepan. Add three sprigs of rosemary, and warm over a medium heat until it starts to bubble. Simmer for 3 minutes or until thickened to a nice consistency. Remove the rosemary sprigs. Strain the sauce using a sieve. Serve warm.

Roast duck Preheat oven to 190°C. Pour out any liquid from inside the duck. Remove the neck (if attached) and close the skin over using cocktail sticks. Trim any excess fat from the main cavity to allow free airflow inside the duck. Do not stuff with anything that would affect airflow. A few leaves of fresh herbs is fine.

For crispy skin, dry the surface of one side of the duck really well with paper towels and rub with salt. Turn duck over and repeat. Place duck on a wire rack in a roasting tray and cook for 40 minutes per kilogram, i.e. 1 hour and 20 minutes for a two-kilogram duck. Halfway through the cooking drain the juices from the tray and set to one side. (This can be used to baste roast potatoes.) Turn the duck and roast for the remaining time. Pierce skin to check that the juices run clear. Remove from oven, cover with foil and rest for 20 minutes before serving.

Serving suggestion
Serve with roast potatoes basted with duck juices and steamed bok choy.

Pairing
The crunchy, oily crust of the skin mixed with the gamey duck meat is delicious. The cherry and rosemary sauce adds an extra, rich dimension that's a delectable sensation. The sparkling shiraz has a blackberry, plum jam aroma, a rich and dense flavour with an overall foamy, sweet and sour sensation. It really washes down the rich and oily duck meat beautifully, counterbalancing the rosemary and complementing the richer components.

Suggested match

Sparkling shiraz, ideally aged

PAIRING STYLE / COMPLEMENTING

CHOCOLATE MOUSSE
with strawberry coulis

No recipe book is complete without a chocolate dessert. I am a certified chocoholic (David's not far behind me) and this mousse is yummy. Using your favourite block of chocolate rather than cooking chocolate adds an extra quality. The most important part is to make sure that the eggs whip to the correct consistency or the mousse won't set correctly. Make sure that your eggs are fresh and that all your equipment is very clean, because even a small contaminant can prevent the egg whites from whisking to a firm froth.

Prep 20 min
Cook 5 min
Set Overnight
Serves
4 large or 6 small

Mousse ingredients

225g (8oz) plain milk chocolate

a knob of butter

3 large eggs, separated and at room temperature

3 tablespoons sugar

⅔ cup (150ml/5oz) thick cream (double/heavy), lightly whipped

50g (1¾oz) dark chocolate, grated

Coulis ingredients

200g (7oz) frozen mixed berries, defrosted

¼ cup (60ml/2fl oz) water

4 tablespoons sugar

Method

Mousse Measure the milk chocolate into a bowl and sit it over a saucepan of simmering water. Melt slowly and make sure the chocolate doesn't overheat or start to bubble. Once melted, remove from the heat and stir in the butter until it has also melted with the chocolate and is fully combined. Let the mixture sit for five minutes and then very gently stir in egg yolks one at a time, until fully combined. Set aside to cool a little. Whip the egg whites and sugar until stiff peaks form. Fold into the chocolate mixture with the whipped cream. Fold gently until all ingredients are fully mixed. Spoon into serving dishes. Transfer to the fridge to set for at least two hours, or overnight for the ideal texture. Top with grated dark chocolate.

Coulis In a medium saucepan combine berries, water and sugar. Bring to a gentle simmer and cook until berries start to disintegrate and sugar is dissolved. Transfer to a blender and mix on high until smooth. Strain through a sieve to remove any seeds. Serve on the side in small bowls.

Pairing

Lambrusco is a sweet sparkling red of charming personality. Try to get one of quality, so that you experience subtlety in the mousse and gentle blackberry and raspberry flavours in the wine. The coulis plays an important role in linking the creamy chocolate with the acidity of the lambrusco. The mousse texture is in synergy with the bead of the wine. It's direct and one-dimensional, but I believe that's part of the beauty of this matching.

Suggested match
Lambrusco

PAIRING STYLE / COMPLEMENTING

CHAMPAGN
BRUT

For a wine to say 'champagne'

on the label it has to have been grown and produced in a very specific region (called Champagne) in France under stringent controls and requirements. Since 1960 nowhere else in the world is allowed lay claim to the title 'champagne', which is why other wines with bubbles are known as 'sparkling' wine.

MENU SUGGESTIONS

Host a gathering with friends or family and invite each guest to bring a specific bottle. Try testing multiple wines with different courses to see how they interact with the various dishes. On the facing page are a few menu suggestions to get you started.

LIGHT AND LUXURIOUS LONG LUNCH

Oysters and foam
w/ blanc de blanc champagne 38

Goats cheese parcels
w/ blanc de blanc champagne 42

Smoked salmon sushi salad
w/ sparkling rosé 98

Chicken tenders
w/ prosecco 68

Cava sorbet
w/ non-vintage cava 56

RICH & DECADENT

Spicy prawn tapas
w/ non-vintage cava 52

Stuffed ricotta mushrooms
w/ dry non-vintage prosecco 66

Roast duck
w/ aged sparkling shiraz 124

Strawberry and moscato cream cakelets
w/ light sparkling moscato 112

DISTINCT PLEASURES

Fondue
w/ vintage New World sparkling 78

Shrimp & pomegranate salad
w/ light sparkling moscato 110

Gnocchi w/asparagus & butter sauce
w/ vintage champagne blend 40

Apple, pear & cinnamon parfait
w/ dry non-vintage prosecco 70

LATINO INFLUENCED

Ceviche
w/ vintage brut cava 54

Manchego cheese croquetas
w/ non-vintage cava 50

Charcuterie
w/ New World brut sparkling rosé 94

Lamb cutlets
w/ non-vintage sparkling shiraz 122

Chocolate mousse
w/ lambrusco 126

ALL THAT SPARKLES

Sushi salad
w/ sparkling rosé 98

Cava sorbet
w/ non-vintage cava 56

Roast duck
w/ aged sparkling shiraz 124

Moscato cakelets
w/ light sparkling moscato 112

Young blue cheese
w/ high quality lambrusco 120

GLOSSARY

A

al dente
Cooking vegetables or pasta to the point that it is still firm when bitten.

AOC/DO/DOC/DOCG, etc
Many wines are produced under strict regulations of quality assurance that are usually defined within a geographical zone.
In English this is known as PDO – Protected Designation of Origin. Each language has a difference acronym for essentially the same meaning, i.e. French (AOC), Spanish (DO/DOCa), Italian (DOC/DOCG), German (QbA/QmP) etc. If you see one of these acronyms on a label you can be assured that the product meets strict requirements to achieve a high standard of quality.

B

blanc de blancs
French wording meaning 'white from white', referring to white wine made from white grapes.

blanc de noirs
French wording meaning 'white from black', referring to white wine made from red grapes.

blend
A term used in winemaking to refer to a mixture of different grape juices selected by a winemaker to create a finished wine.

body
A term used in winemaking to refer to the sensation of weight in the liquid. Wine has a varying viscosity depending on the alcohol content, similar to the difference between skimmed and full-cream milk.

Brachetto d'Acqui
A lightly sparkling (or still) red Italian wine from the Piedmont region, made from the brachetto grape.

brut
A term used to describe a wine as dry in style.

burrata
A fresh soft Italian cheese with rich buttery flavour, with a firm shell and oozing interior.

C

cabernet franc
A red wine variety from Bordeaux in France with a lighter style than cabernet sauvignon.

cakelet
A slang term used to describe a small cake.

calamari
Cooked squid (usually fried) cut into pieces, often rings.

cap classique
South African sparkling wine.

cava
Spanish sparkling wine.

caviar
Edible delicacy of fish eggs (roe).

ceviche
Fresh seafood dish, made from raw fish cured in citrus juices, popular in the Americas.

champagne
Sparkling wine produced in the Champagne region of France.

charcuterie
A term used to encompass a broad range of cured/preserved meat products such as salamis, smoked hams, terrine, pâtés etc.

chardonnay
A popular white wine grape variety.

charmat method
A term used to describe a method of winemaking that – among other techniques – utilises stainless steel tanks during the fermentation process.

cheddar
An English cheese variety with a firm texture that varies in intensity of flavour and colour depending on the addition of spices.

chenin blanc
A white wine variety of high acidity originating from the Loire Valley in France.

chèvre
Goat's cheese, usually with a salty soft texture although many variations are available.

chinese cabbage
A vegetable often used in Asian cuisine, also known as napa cabbage. Not to be confused with bok choy.

coriander
An edible herb also known as cilantro, with a sharp citrus flavour.

coulis
A thick strongly flavoured sauce made from puréed and strained fruit.

coupe
A shallow bowl-shaped stemmed glass designed to serve champagne, however more often used nowadays for cocktails.

crémant
A particular style of French sparkling wine produced outside of the region of Champagne.

cru/premier cru/grand cru
A French wine term used to describe a winemaking region, often of high quality.

cuvée (meaning blend)
also prestige cuvée/cuvée spéciale
Cuvée in champagne usually refers to the highest quality juice that comes from the first gentle grape pressing. Used in conjunction with the words 'prestige' or 'spéciale' it can mean a particularly high quality blend, but care should be taken if used with other words, that it's not just marketing spin.

D

demi-sec
A term used to describe a wine as sweet in style.

doux
A term used to describe a wine as very sweet in style.

dukkah
A dip of finely ground herbs, spices and/or nuts originating from Egypt.

E

échelle de crus
From French meaning 'ladder of growth', referring to a scale used to define quality of location for growing Champagne grapes.

edam
A semi-hard cheese from Edam in the Netherlands with a mild flavour that sharpens with age.

edamame
Green soybeans boiled in the pod and usually served salted.

empanada
Stuffed, folded pastry pie popular in Latin America. Favourite fillings include meats and cheese.

extra brut
A term used to describe a wine as extremely dry in style.

extra dry
Paradoxically, a term used to describe a wine as off-dry rather than extra dry in style.

F

fermentation
The process of converting grape juice to alcohol, using yeast to convert natural sugars to alcohol.

fetta
A white, soft, brined, crumbly cheese originating from Greece.

fondue (cheese)
A dish of melted cheese, used for dipping selective items like bread, meats, vegetable etc. originating in Switzerland.

Franciacorta
A wine region in Lombardy, Italy, that produces sparkling wine.

frizzante
An Italian wine term meaning lightly sparkling.

G

gherkins
A small cucumber-like vegetable that is usually pickled.

glera
A white Italian grape variety used to create prosecco wine.

gouda
A popular firm cheese from the Netherlands. Taste varies depending on age.

grand cru
A regional wine classification. In the case of champagne it refers to the top 9% of vineyard land.

gruyère
A sweet but slightly salty hard cheese from Switzerland.

H

halloumi
A hard salty cheese from Cyprus that is often grilled or fried.

I, J,K,L

injection method/carbonation
A term used to describe a cheap method of winemaking that involves adding bubbles synthetically to sparkling wine.

jamón serrano
A Spanish cured ham that is usually served in very thin slices.

lambrusco
A light and lightly sparkling red wine from Italy.

M

macabeo
A Spanish grape variety used in the production of Cava.

manchego
A firm Spanish cheese made from sheep's milk.

marinade
A herbal and/or seasoned liquid used to soak meat or fish in cooking to enhance flavour.

marinate
A verb used to describe the process of creating a marinade.

merlot
A red wine grape variety that is produced alone or as part of a blend.

méthode traditionnelle (traditional method, méthode champenoise or classic method)
A term used to describe a method of winemaking that – among other techniques – utilises strict growing, pruning, processing and winemaking techniques as well as a second fermentation in the bottle.

meunier
A black grape most notable for its use in the production of champagne.

monteray jack
A mild semi-hard cheese made with cow's milk from America.

mozzarella
A semi-soft cheese traditionally made from buffalo milk in Italy or cow's milk in other places.

N

New World
In relation to wine, this term refers to locations that have been planted with vines after European immigrants discovered the various territories, including America, Argentina, Australia, Chile and New Zealand. More recently the UK, India and China have also become New World producers.

non-vintage
The majority of sparkling wine is non-vintage, i.e. the blend can be made of juice from harvests of multiple years.

O, P

parmesan
(parmigiano-reggiano in Italy)
A hard, richly flavoured cheese from Italy, which is often grated to dress a meal.

parellada
A Spanish grape variety used in the production of cava.

pâté
A paste or terrine made from meat products and seasonings, often including liver.

pecorino
An Italian hard cheese with a mild buttery flavour made from sheep's milk.

pepperoni
An American spicy cured meat inspired by Italian salamis.

petit syrah
A red wine variety from the Rhône region in France with high alcohol and rich tannins.

pinot noir
A difficult to grow, red grape variety that is produced worldwide but has a particular association with Burgundy in France. It is also used in a champagne blend.

pomegranate
A fruit consisting of hundreds of tightly compacted juicy edible seeds encased in a tough skin.

prosciutto
An Italian, dry-cured, thinly sliced ham.

prosecco
A light, fresh sparkling white wine made from glera grapes, originating from Italy.

Q, R

queso fresco
A creamy, soft, mild white cheese, popular in Latin American countries.

reserve
A term used in winemaking to define a portion of high quality juice put aside to age before it is incorporated in a blend. Since this is an unregulated term, it can also be purely a marketing ploy.

ricotta
A light creamy Italian cheese created from the whey left over from producing other cheeses.

rosé
A still or sparkling style of wine with a pink colour due to contact with red grape skins or the addition of a small portion of red wine.

S

sabrage
A dramatic technique for opening a bottle of champagne with a sword (sabre) for ceremonial purposes, which originated in the Napolean era.

sauvignon blanc
A popular white wine variety produced around the world but particularly associated with New Zealand.

sec
A term used to describe a wine as lightly sweet in style.

sekt
German sparkling wine.

sopressata
An Italian dry salami that can be found in a number of styles.

spumante
Italian term to describe sparkling wine.

sushi
A Japanese cuisine that usually includes rice with raw sliced fish and some vegetables.

T

terrine
A terrine is a seasoned meat loaf similar to a pâté, however larger and the ingredients are more coarsely chopped.

terroir
A wine term used to encompass the environment, soil type, growing conditions and climate during grape growing for wine.

tobiko
A Japanese term to describe the bright orange roe of a flying fish, which looks similar to caviar.

transfer method
Similar to the traditional winemaking method, until the final stage, when some processes are completed more economically in bulk rather than in the bottle, which is very time consuming.

U, V, W, X, Y, Z

vintage
Vintage sparkling wine is usually produced from the grapes from a single harvest recognised for excellent growing conditions.

xarel·lo
A Spanish grape variety used in the production of Cava.

zest
A food ingredient created by grating the external skin of citrus fruit.

CONVERSION TABLES

We have included a wide range of measurement formats throughout our recipes to make them easily accessible to as wide an audience as possible, but there are always additional considerations. Here are a few extra conversions:

CELSIUS TO GAS MARK

110°C	=	¼
130°C	=	½
140°C	=	1
150°C	=	2
170°C	=	3
180°C	=	4
190°C	=	5
200°C	=	6
220°C	=	7
230°C	=	8
240°C	=	9
250°C	=	10

CUPS TO GRAMS

breadcrumbs
1 cup = 70g

caster sugar (superfine)
1 cup = 220g

parmesan cheese, grated
1 cup = 80g

flour
1 cup = 150g

REGIONAL TERMINOLOGY FOR INGREDIENTS

caster sugar	=	superfine sugar
coriander	=	cilantro
cos lettuce	=	romaine lettuce
cornflour	=	corn starch
spring onion	=	green onion or scallion
plain flour	=	all-purpose flour

CAUTION

Some of the recipes that are included in this book use raw egg, alcohol, marinated fish or unpasteurised cheeses.

Pregnant women, young children and anyone not in full health should use caution or avoid these ingredients.

Please always use very fresh ingredients and excellent kitchen hygiene.

INDEX

RECIPES AT A GLANCE

BY COURSE

RECIPES AT A GLANCE

BY MAIN INGREDIENT

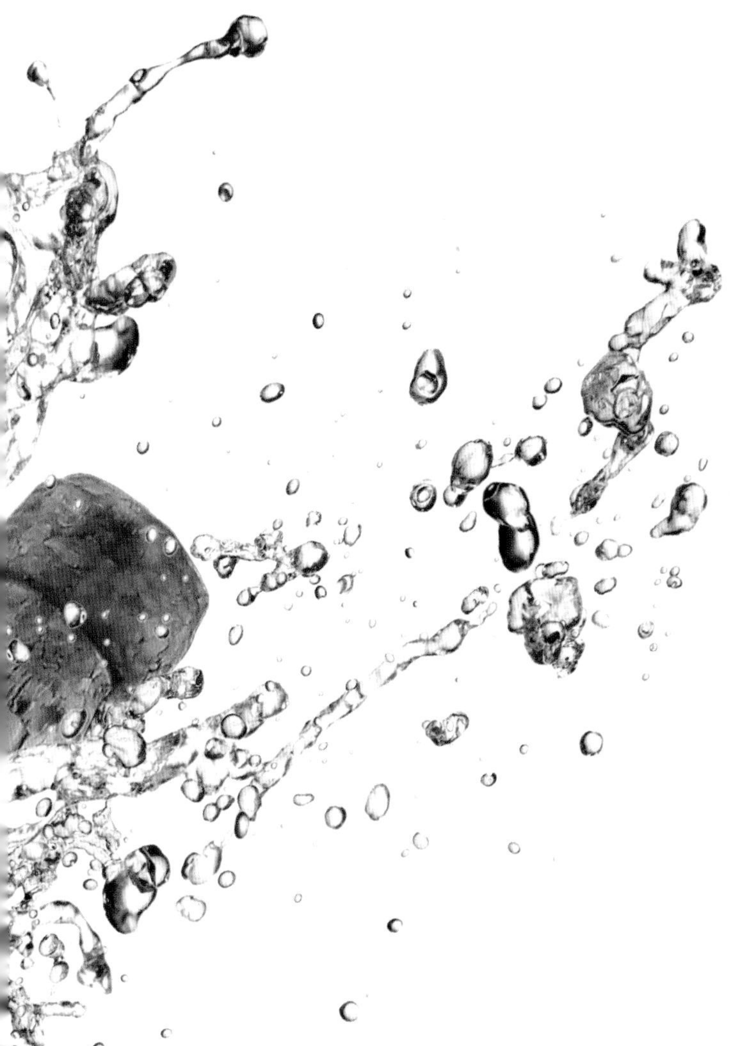

The glass of a champagne or sparkling wine *bottle has to be much thicker than a normal wine bottle in order to withstand the pressure of the sparkling wine. It generates a load that is equivalent to the pressure in a bus tyre, which is three times the pressure in a standard car tyre. This force propels the cork from the bottle at almost 100kmph (60mph).*

FUTURE EDITIONS

PAIRED – *Champagne & Sparkling Wines* is the first in a series of books. We already have two further volumes in the planning stages, PAIRED – *Whites* and PAIRED – *Reds,* and a wealth of additional ideas beyond these volumes. All books will be available in hardback and ebook format. Keep in touch with us on social media or via our email newsletter to find out in advance of new releases as well as to receive introductory discounts.

If you have suggestions for inclusions in future volumes we would be delighted to receive your recommendations. Indeed, all comments and constructive feedback regarding this volume, which will be regularly revised, will be gratefully received also.

CONNECT WITH US

Website
www.paired-media.com

Email
publisher@paired-media.com

Social media
Facebook /pairedmedia
Instagram @paired_media
Twitter @paired_media

Fran Flynn is a commercial photographer and graphic designer. You can make an enquiry regarding your photography and/or graphic design project through her business Frangipani Creative. www.frangipanicreative.com

David Stevens-Castro offers a variety of services related to wine, including event presentation, wine education, wine buying, fine wine consulting, wine list creation, etc. You can contact him via publisher@paired-media.com or on social media.

ACKNOWLEDGEMENTS

This has been a labour of love from beginning to end. There is nothing better than working on what you enjoy – work disappears and is replaced by pleasure. While we produced this book essentially between the two of us, there are several very important people to thank for their contributions.

Tyson Stelzer's exceptionally generous support and endorsement is hugely appreciated. Martine Lleonart has been a fantastic editor that we highly recommend.

Sarah DeNardi is a brilliant food stylist who often works with Fran, and has been very generous with tips and support during the production of this book, which was styled by Fran.

Special thanks to Rob and Melinda Buker at Burleigh on View, Burleigh Heads, who provided us with the lovely white kitchen location. For accommodation enquires please call 0414 258 855.

We would also like to acknowledge Andrew Dorenburg and Karen Page, who don't actually know us, but have written an incredibly deep book *What to Drink with What you Eat*, which has been an invaluable reference for us when considering pairing ideas and developing our recipes.

On a more personal level, Barbara helped us so much with entertaining our little boy when we needed to work, as well as Johanna and Gaby. Katie was a great help (and spontaneous assistant photographer) during some beach shots also.

Both of our families have been endlessly supportive of our endeavours, both financially and emotionally, so we would like to say a massive thank you to all of you. A special mention has to be made of Frank Flynn, who isn't here to see this project come to life, but who always offered enormous support and encouragement and who is missed more than words can express.

Food and wine matching is a subjective art. It is also a pleasure available to everyone and should be enjoyed without fear or pretension.

Leave your comfort zone behind, try the unexpected and bask in discoveries that your taste buds will be forever grateful for.